By Ernest Hemingway

HEMINGWAY LIBRARY EDITIONS

The Sun Also Rises
A Farewell to Arms
For Whom the Bell Tolls
The Old Man and the Sea
Green Hills of Africa

NOVELS

The Torrents of Spring
The Sun Also Rises
A Farewell to Arms
To Have and Have Not
For Whom the Bell Tolls
Across the River and into the Trees
The Old Man and the Sea
Islands in the Stream
The Garden of Eden
True at First Light

STORIES

In Our Time
Men Without Women
Winner Take Nothing
*The Fifth Column and Four Stories
of the Spanish Civil War*

*The Short Stories of Ernest
Hemingway*
*The Snows of Kilimanjaro and
Other Stories*
The Nick Adams Stories
*The Complete Short Stories of
Ernest Hemingway*

NONFICTION

Death in the Afternoon
Green Hills of Africa
Selected Letters 1917–1961
On Writing
A Moveable Feast
The Dangerous Summer
Dateline: Toronto
By-Line: Ernest Hemingway
*A Moveable Feast: The Restored
Edition*

ANTHOLOGIES

Hemingway on Fishing
Hemingway on Hunting
Hemingway on War

DEAR PAPA

The Letters of
Patrick and Ernest Hemingway

Prologue and Epilogue by

PATRICK

HEMINGWAY

Edited by

BRENDAN HEMINGWAY

AND STEPHEN ADAMS

SCRIBNER

New York   London   Toronto   Sydney   New Delhi

Scribner
An Imprint of Simon & Schuster, Inc.
1230 Avenue of the Americas
New York, NY 10020

First Scribner hardcover edition June 2022

SCRIBNER and design are registered trademarks of The Gale Group, Inc.,
used under license by Simon & Schuster, Inc., the publisher of this work.

For information about special discounts for bulk purchases, please contact Simon &
Schuster Special Sales at 1-866-506-1949 or business@simonandschuster.com.

The Simon & Schuster Speakers Bureau can bring authors to your live event. For more
information or to book an event, contact the Simon & Schuster Speakers Bureau
at 1-866-248-3049 or visit our website at www.simonspeakers.com.

Interior design by Laura Levatino

Manufactured in the United States of America

1 3 5 7 9 10 8 6 4 2

Library of Congress Cataloging-in-Publication Data

Names: Hemingway, Ernest, 1899–1961. Correspondence. Selections. |
Hemingway, Patrick. Correspondence. Selections. | Hemingway, Brendan,
editor. | Adams, Stephen, 1990– editor.
Title: Dear Papa : the letters of Patrick and Ernest Hemingway / prologue and epilogue by
Patrick Hemingway ; edited by Brendan Hemingway and Stephen Adams. Description: First
Scribner hardcover edition. | New York : Scribner, 2022. | Includes index.
Identifiers: LCCN 2022002400 (print) | LCCN 2022002401 (ebook) | ISBN
9781982196868 (hardcover) | ISBN 9781982196875 (ebook)
Subjects: LCSH: Hemingway, Ernest, 1899–1961—Correspondence. | Hemingway,
Patrick—Correspondence. | Novelists, American—20th
century—Correspondence. | LCGFT: Personal correspondence.
Classification: LCC PS3515.E37 Z48 2022 (print) | LCC PS3515.E37 (ebook)
| DDC 813/.52 [B]—dc23/eng/20220316
LC record available at https://lccn.loc.gov/2022002400
LC ebook record available at https://lccn.loc.gov/2022002401

ISBN 978-1-9821-9686-8
ISBN 978-1-9821-9687-5 (ebook)

CONTENTS

PROLOGUE

THIS BOOK contains selected conversations, by letter, between a father and son. It is an attempt to answer the question I have been often asked, by friends and strangers alike: "Did I know my father?"

There is a lot of hunting and fishing in these letters, but I think the significance of this correspondence is not the hunting and fishing. It's the light it casts on our relationship, and how I grew to know my father. I grew to know him as a person, quite different than how he is often portrayed. The man I knew tried very hard to be a good family man. I think our correspondence shows he was intimately connected with his wives and his children all his life.

I would like to call up a letter by my father that he wrote to F. Scott Fitzgerald in 1925, when Papa had only one family and marriage to play with.

July 1, 1925
Burguete, Navarra

Dear Scott,

We are going in to Pamplona tomorrow. Been trout fishing here. How are you? And how is Zelda?

PROLOGUE

I am feeling better than I've ever felt haven't drunk any thing but wine since I left Paris. God it has been wonderful country. But you hate country. All right omit description of country. I wonder what your idea of heaven would be. A beautiful vacuum filled with wealthy monogamists, all powerful and members of the best families all drinking themselves to death. And hell would probably be an ugly vacuum full of poor polygamists unable to obtain booze or with chronic stomach disorders that they called secret sorrows.

To me a heaven would be a big bull ring with me holding two barrera seats and a trout stream outside that no one else was allowed to fish in and two lovely houses in the town; one where I would have my wife and children and be monogamous and love them truly and well and the other where I would have my nine beautiful mistresses on 9 different floors and one house would be fitted up with special copies of the Dial printed on soft tissue and kept in the toilets on every floor and in the other house we would use the American Mercury and the New Republic. Then there would be a fine church like in Pamplona where I could go and be confessed on the way from one house to the other and I would get on my horse and ride out with my son to my bull ranch named Hacienda Hadley and toss coins to all my illegitimate children that lined the road. I would write out at the Hacienda and send my son in to lock the chastity belts onto my mistresses because someone had just galloped up with the news that a notorious monogamist named Fitzgerald had been seen riding toward the town at the head of a company of strolling drinkers.

Well anyway we're going into town tomorrow early in the morning. Write me at the

Hotel Quintana

Pamplona

Spain

Or don't you like to write letters. I do because it's such a swell way to keep from working and yet feel you've done something.

So long and love to Zelda from us both.

> Yours,
> Ernest

This letter demonstrates Ernest's complex personality and his ability to create art with his writing. As my maturity developed, I too could use my letters to create something similar to his and in certain fields, such as poetry and hunting, I could openly compete. This letter to Fitzgerald was written three years before I was born and John Hadley Nicanor Hemingway was Papa's only son and child. My appearance on the scene, the son of Pauline Pfeiffer Hemingway, altered the complexity of the family Papa had to deal with. This complexity also affected the development of the letters between Papa and me. In the first place, there was the matter of the Catholic Church. Papa had entered into a relationship with the Catholic Church during the war that was fought in Italy, a strongly Catholic country. With his second marriage to Pauline, he would become very much under the influence of her religion, and I would be brought up as a Catholic child. This relationship in turn would be affected by Papa and Pauline's divorce in order for him to marry Martha Gellhorn. These changes that Papa had to make in the families he felt responsible for, very much underlie the trajectory of our correspondence and the task of getting to know my father.

Patrick Hemingway

INTRODUCTION

DEAR PAPA is a look into the intimate relationship between Ernest Hemingway and his middle son, Patrick. It is an abridged collection of the correspondence that they maintained throughout their lives together.

Patrick Hemingway started the Dear Papa project in 2020 when he enlisted the help of both his nephew, Brendan Hemingway, and his grandson, Stephen Adams. Patrick's intention was to use the large archive of this material to show the world what his parent was like as a father.

The world already knows Ernest Hemingway the writer and Papa Hemingway the larger-than-life celebrity. Now Patrick wants the world to know the devoted family man and engaged father by sharing selected letters over their entire collective life together.

Ernest Hemingway was married four times and had three children between two of his four wives, so the supporting cast in these letters is large. He married Hadley Richardson in 1921, and they divorced in 1927. Hadley was the mother of Patrick's beloved older brother, Jack, but she would not play much of a role in Patrick's life. Patrick and his brother Gregory's mother, Pauline Pfeiffer, was married to Hemingway 1927–1940. She was a constant in Patrick's life until her untimely death in 1951, when Patrick was twenty-three years old. Martha "Marty" Gellhorn married Hemingway in 1940, and they divorced in 1945. Martha was especially fond of Patrick, and the two remained in contact for the rest of Martha's life. And in 1946, Hemingway married Mary Welsh, who was widowed by his death in 1961. Although Patrick was nearly eighteen years old when Mary married Ernest, they developed a cordial relationship and shared a keen interest in art history.

As Ernest's middle son, Patrick was the stereotypically dutiful peacemaking middle child who kept in touch with his father until his father's death. They corresponded through thick and thin, always making it through rough patches in their relationship in a way that was not typical for Ernest, who tended to withdraw from confrontation and retreat from high emotion.

In addition to the large cast of characters, many of these characters are referred to by nicknames. The Hemingway family have long had a tradition of nicknames, and Ernest was particularly good at it and into it.

Another family tradition you will observe in the letters is the "toosie," which is a way to represent a kiss: a circle with a dot in it, which we usually typeset as "(.)." Ernest inherited this tradition and passed it on.

Neither father nor son was much for spelling, so many errors have been fixed to avoid interfering with the reading experience.

When we say "letters," we mean all the correspondence, which included not only letters but telegrams, postcards, and short notes.

As we reviewed the letters in 2020, they were between eighty-eight years old and fifty-nine years old. Language and stereotyping that was commonplace then is recognized as harmful now. Patrick was adamant that there was to be no whitewashing, so none of the problematic words or phrases he or his father used in their letters have been left out. No excuses will be made. There are also graphic depictions of hunting and fishing that some readers may find unsavory. Our goal is historical accuracy. We apologize in advance to anyone who is put off by the raw nature of this text.

We had access to the entire archive thanks to Sandra Spanier of the Hemingway Letters Project and the wonderful personnel at JFK Presidential Library and Museum (where they preserve the Ernest Hemingway Collection). In addition to providing access to the material, they helped us by providing missing documents and transcribing damaged or incomplete papers.

The result is a collection of selected letters, in chronological order, grouped into broad periods of Patrick's life.

We hope that this curated glimpse into the correspondence between father and son will broaden and deepen the Hemingway fan's understanding of the man beyond the author.

Brendan Hemingway & Stephen Adams

PART I: EARLY CHILDHOOD

WHEN PATRICK was born in June 1928, Ernest Hemingway was twenty-eight years old. He had already published *The Sun Also Rises* (1926), and *A Farewell to Arms* was about to be released. Ernest wrote his first letter to Patrick when he was just four years old. Ernest was on his first African safari, which would ignite a lifelong passion for that continent. Patrick was coping with having a younger brother, Gregory, born in November 1931.

While there are relatively few letters from this period, they represent the foundation of a relationship which was deep and significant to both father and son. In an article in *Playboy*, published in December of 1968, Patrick would refer to his childhood as "truly magical," and from these letters we can see why.

When Patrick wrote the last letter in this section, he was just shy of fourteen years old, romping around Key West, enjoying the last of his pre–boarding school freedom. Ernest was hunting U-boats in Cuba.

THE FIRST LETTER

To Patrick Hemingway,
August 12, 1932
L Bar T Ranch, Wyoming

Dear Patrick:

How are you and how is Hooley and Gregory?

Papa took mama down to go to church and we went shooting too. We shot 24 Sage hens. They are bigger than chickens and fly very fast and make a big roar when they fly. We have eaten nearly all of them and eat the rest tomorrow. My they are good!

Coming home we saw 4 bears and 4 big bull moose. I took their pictures and when they are done will send them to you.

Every night we hear the coyotes howl.

Papa has been sick in bed but he is all right now.

When my book comes out next month I will send it to you for you alone. It has fine pictures.

Tell Aunt Jinny I am trying to buy a good pointer to hunt with Hooley.

from Papa

Love to Everybody at Piggott in your house

TRIP TO AFRICA, 1934

To PH, January 19, 1934
Nairobi, Kenya

Dear old Mex:

How are you old Booze fighter?

Give my best to Mr. Josie and Capt. Bra and Sully.

Tell Griggy his mother is a great hunter.

You should have seen the natives carry her on their shoulders chanting and dancing and singing the lion song the night we killed our first big lion. They carried her around the fire and all the way to her tent.

We have seen 83 lions We killed 3 black maned lions. Big ones. Charles killed the biggest. And one other lion. Then we killed 35 hyenas. 3 Buffalo bulls. About 8 Thompson gazelles, about Six Grant Gazelles, 3 Topi, 4 Eland, 6 Impalla, 2 Leopards, 5 Cheetah, a lot of Zebra for their hides. 3 Water buck, one cerval cat, 1 bush buck, 1 Roan Antelope, 3 wart hogs, 2 Klipspringers, 2 oribi, and I don't know how many sand grouse, ducks, lesser bustard and greater bustard and partridges.

You would love this country.

Maybe we will come out here and live all of us. Mother likes it the best of any place she's ever been.

I got amoebic dysentery on the boat and had to fly in 400 miles in a little plane ordered by the government fellers in Lake Victoria

Nyanza to see a Dr. He has fixed me up, with injections, and I fly back day after tomorrow.

When I was sick [MISSING TEXT, MARGIN CUT OFF] a pint of blood at grand commission every day.

I thought my insides were coming out and that we would have to put in some of Jimmy's old hose.

Give my love to your Aunt Ura and tell her I'll write her. Also love to Beezer, to Griggy and best regards to Ada. (.)

Also remember me to Jimmy. (.)

Please write us.

Love from Papa (.)

A PICNIC AND ILL WILL TOWARD A ROOSTER

To Ernest Hemingway, August 16, 1939 (age 11)
Summer Camp, Vermont

Dear Papa

How are you. I got your letter day before yesterday. Please bring the air rifle out west. Yesterday we went on a picnic to the Kahns we had hambergers and after that we went to the brook and had a swim. Today is field day we are going to have all kinds of sports we are all fine.

love Patrick

x x x x x x x x x x

p.s. hope the rooster is dead.

NEWS FROM HOME

To PH, August 23, 1939
Key West, Florida

Dearest Mouse and Giggy;

Well we got back to Key West all right but it certainly is lonesome with no family. Had to cross in a bad blow and my legs still ache from steering all night. Too rough to sit on the seat and the sea abeam (sideways), so it was all roll.

The place is fine. Six banties still alive. Peacocks killed some. All hen peacocks have chicks. Hen peacocks have no tails. Jimmy has no tobacco Mr. Ernest.

Mother writes she is having a wonderful time. She has been in Germany and Austria too and all over France in a car.

Have to stop now for packing. Everybody from here sends love to you. Either Bruce or I will pick you up. Probably Bruce as I do not want to face New York with all business to do as well as the Stork Club to look after when should get out to the ranch.

74,000 words done on the book. I was sitting with prickly heat writing about a snowstorm and it was getting more difficult and more difficult and so I thought, "What the what citizens let's go out west and see a snowstorm."

Be very good with Bruce on the train and not be nuisances because being all by ourselves everybody has to be as good as possible or we will be liable to have the glorious discipline of indiscipline and you remember where that got the Spanish Republic to. (That well known Creek.)

Much love from Papa and see you soonest. Have the Air rifle and so on. The Bumby caught a big rainbow trout, he writes, in the North Fork of Shoshoni.

Papa (.) (.) (.) (.) (.) (.) (.) (.)

TICKER TROUBLE

To PH, late April 1940
Finca Vigía, Cuba

Dearest Mouse:

Thanks for the good letter. You write better all the time.

The weather is fine here today and if Uncle Leicester doesn't come today I am going to be afraid that he and Sir Anthony have ticker trouble. There have been three good days now to cross. But no sign of them.

Do you know what ticker trouble is? Fighters call the heart the ticker and ticker trouble is sometimes spoken of as lack of moxie. Do you know what Moxie is? Moxie is what our banty rooster has plenty of.

Glad they've got some good fights. Has Geech fought? Or the Iron Baby? Or Lord Joseph the Fighting Bob of Battles?

Here we've won the last eight times straight at Pelota and I am way ahead on the season. Over 100 dollars ahead. Ermua has been playing wonderfully and so has Guillermo. Guillermo comes out to the house now to play tennis too. He can play with either his right or his left hand and can serve faster than Sir Anthony even.

Papa is down to 198 lbs and in very good shape. Yesterday I borrowed Frankie Steinhardt's pointer Vicky and hunted way into the back country. It is beautiful there. Plenty of doves and Galdings along the stream we found one covey of quail. Also three jack snipe. Also pointed an unknown something and when I walked in to kick it out what should it be but a setting hen. I know all the people on the land back of us almost to our Old church so you can hunt wherever you want to.

Shot three guineas last week. Am not shooting too many because want there to be plenty when you come. Am getting some pigeons too and letting them go wild. The guineas are wonderful to shoot flying. As good as pheasants. I got one with the right barrel and one with the left barrel as the whole flock came over me at the height of the big tree tops. When they hit the ground they really make a bump too.

Everybody asks about you and when you are coming back. Haven't let anybody shoot a plover on the place and there are plenty of them now. The jack snipe are funny. Sometimes there will be as many as a dozen on the bog. Then you won't find one. Yesterday one I got was only stunned by one pellet. You could have had him for a pet. But instead he became a thing for the stomach. That dog pointed them beautifully. The other day when had no dog there was a whole covey of quail dusting in the road. They wouldn't fly and ran into the brush before they went up. There were about thirty in the covey and I didn't get one because from the brush they flew across the river.

Tell Giggy to write. Much love old Mouse.

(.) (.) (.) **Papa** (.) (.) (.)

Book goes good. Have 28 chapters done.
Dr. Kohly sends his best. He is anxious to see you and see how the treatment is coming. Are you keeping up your Tennis?

PIRATE'S COVE

To EH, May 30, 1942 (age 13)
Key West, Florida

Dear Papa,

School lets out the end of next week, we are coming over the following week, depending when we can get reservations.

Mother got back Thursday from her trip to Piggott. She lost five pounds and looks very well. Gregory is just recovering from a cold, the first one since we saw you.

Gregory and I and a couple of other boys, rode up to Pirates Cove on our bycycles, we fished up there on the old railroad bridge. I caught nothing, but Cort (one of the boys that went with us), caught a big snapper and a grouper.

Most of the birds have gone north now, but we still have a few. So far I have an average of 94% in exams, I hope I keep it up. Ada and I are okay.

The bantam hen brought out two chicks, out of twelve eggs, not so hot. They are very cute, one is much darker than the other. Both roosters go around arguing which one is the father.

I have been doing a lot of fishing, mostly for snappers and jacks. I use live shrimps for the snappers, plugs for jacks. Grand total so far; one barracuda, lots of bait.

The woodworms are swarming now, you can hardly stay near a light.

Gas rationing has gone into effect. Mother can get only 3 gallons a week.

How is Bumby.

Give love to Marty.

Love
Mouse

PART II: BOARDING SCHOOL

PATRICK ATTENDED Canterbury School in New Milford, Connecticut, from fall 1942 until spring 1946. When he went off to boarding school, he was fourteen years old and Ernest was forty-three years old.

Patrick started his boarding school career quite homesick for the freedom and fun of roaming all over Key West with the local pack of boys or enjoying Cuba with his family. He missed the tropical weather as well.

Worse still, life went on without him: his father continued to hunt U-boats at this time (referred to as "scientific work" in the letters to avoid censorship), and then Ernest went to cover the war in Europe while Patrick had to stay behind. We benefit from the resulting letters, but young Patrick felt that he was missing out.

However, by the time Patrick graduated from Canterbury, he was well past being homesick and ready to spread his wings a bit.

THE TRIP TO SCHOOL

To EH, undated, late summer 1942
Canterbury School, New Milford, CT

Dear Papa,

I had a fine trip over from Cuba, they put up those screens when we took off, when we flew off Key West, and when we landed, so I did not see much on the trip.

Miami has improved (a lot) since the war, most of the Jews have pulled out. The Miami Colonial Hotel has gone to pot, no service, no nothin'.

The trip up on the train was uneventful, except in some city in South Carolina, when hundreds of soldiers mobbed the train, they were on leave, but had no places, so decided to stand it anyway.

New York is about the same as ever, there aren't so many cars, and the hotel service is bad but all together it's about the same.

I have got a lot of new clothes, all pretty hot and uncomfortable. How I wish I could wear Cuba clothes.

I had to have a check up before school, it seems I have nothing the matter with me, except a slight thyroid defishency (my own spelling) tell Marty I'll have to get together with her and celebrate.

Give Wolf Man my love, I was very disappointed he couldn't make it.

How is the scientific work coming along?

Give Gigi love, and tell him I will write him a long comic tragic letter on school life.

Has Marty gotten back?

Hope you are all having a good time. Tell Mr. Shevilean I delivered his message, and it was heartily appreciated.

Looking forward to school

Love Patrick

WOLFER (THE CAT)

To PH, September 23, 1942
Finca Vigía, Cuba

Dearest Mouse:

It certainly has been negligent of us men not to have written before but the factory has been going at such speed that. Every time would sit down someone else would need typewriter.

Boy it was quiet and lonesome after you left. Not even the Wolfman could cheer us up. He felt plenty gloomy too that you were gone. Winston didn't leave till after the Holyfathers Special left from Grand Central; that's why you didn't see him in N.Y.

Now let's see what news. Won is due to come back down here the tenth or fifteenth. May be some delay due to so much work piled up in the fiction factory.

Wolfer, the cat Mayito gave us, a big Persian, strong as a bull, ten months old and coloured like a snow leopard. Giggy took a pretty good picture of him with the kodack which we are enclosing. He is a good outdoors cat.

Had two shoots since you left and I won 78 and 86. Giggy split two ten buck miss and out pools last time; one with Quintero; one with me and on his side bets won six bucks more to turn in a nice 36 bucks win. He has well over 60 now. Giggy, Papa and Wolfer beat Torlio, Shevlin and Rodriguez Diaz. Giggy and I shot straight and the Wolf dropped one bird.

Marty got back; but she'll write you her news.

Do they have censorship of your mail at school or is it o.k. to make an occasional joke?

I have done nothing but work in the factory. Sometimes from 5 in the morning until 11 at night. Books coming along fine.

Wasn't it terrible about the Dodgers.

Have it fixed up to get out in boat for scientific collecting for the Museum. We bought a stout 18 foot sailing boat too in Cojimar and rigged her up for a fighting fish chair. So even when no gas you can always get down to where the goggle fishing is and sail back. It's a fine big comfortable Cojimar marlin fishing boat; built new this year, with new sails, oars and masts. That way you will never be without a boat. Get permit for Pilar too.

Mouse old pal I have to stop now. Get to work. Everybody sends their best love. I'm having Janes Aircraft of The World sent you. It's a late and huge book. Make it a going away to school present. I love you very much and miss you like the devil. Sure school is fine. Awfully anxious to hear.

>   Much love from
>   Papa
>
>   Ernest Hemingway.

A LOT LIKE IDAHO

To EH, September 27, 1942
Canterbury School

Dear Papa,

I am very sorry I did not write you sooner, but every thing takes so much time that I have only time to write one letter a week.

I am having a very good time here, it is three times the school I thought it was.

I am having quite a time with my lessons but I am getting along better. French and Latin are giving me quite a bit of trouble, but Algebra, history & English are simple enough so far.

I got a fine letter from Wolfman in which he told me all his news, but I haven't gotten a letter from you yet, did you you get my letter?

I was very glad to hear Gigi got over his sickness so soon. How is Tester's kitten?

How is the scientific expedition coming along, have you found any young marlin, have you got the extra equipment?

The country around here is very nice, a lot like Idaho, if I wasn't go to school I'd like it very much.

Wolfman invited me to Gardners Island when I can come, but I don't no when I can make it.

I am trying out for the midgets (first year football) I think I may make the first string because of a very fortunated incident, a guy named King, and I were playing guards in a skrimmage in which the first string was supposed to swarm over us, they did not make a yard in four downs. The reasons for this was they left a very big hole in front of both of us every time, so that we were able to tackle the runner very quickly. Hope they don't find out I don't know how many men there are on a football team.

I hope I will hear from you soon. I sorry there isn't more news, but every thing is so routine in a boarding school, as you well know, Love, Mouse PS Give Gigi much love and tell him I'll write him within the week.

THANKSGIVING CANCELED?

To EH, October 5, 1942
Canterbury School

Dear Papa,

Thank you very much for the letter. I was getting quite lonesome.

School gets funnier and better every day, there is no censorship here so you can make jokes.

There sure are some super fakes here, Master Manupelli I think comes first on the list. He is the greatest hunter in the world, his favorite duck to shoot is Black Duck, but when I showed him a picture of them, he thought it was a pintail.

My school is coming along very well except, as I told you before, my French which is horrible, 25%, 50%, 10% are average for my papers. I don't have any trouble with my pronounciation, but I just can't remember the grammer but I am trying hard, and maybe I will improve.

I am now first string guard on the midgets, but I am a jibering wreck, my wrist is ruined, my ankles are all shot and I can hard walk, football's a wonderful game, groan.

I have not heard anything from Bumby, have you?

The boys here are certainly strong here, this morning at mass, three boys were carried out in a dead faint, and half of the rest were sick.

I wonder if you might order me some books, there is nothing here to read but funny books, and I don't care for them so much any more.

Gigi would like it here very much, there are more Yankee fans here than I have ever seen collected under one roof in my life.

I am sorry if I sound so critical but I am getting kind of sick of school in general, it's so much like camp, with a little more routine, but then nothing is gained without effort, and boy what effort.

There are lots of birds around here, but I don't have much time to see them.

I was very happy to get Gigi's letter, I miss him very much.

We are not going to have any Thanksgiving vacation, and even Doc. Hume, the headmaster, doesn't know when the Christmas vacation will be. I wish you would write him a letter asking him about it by air mail, it might help. But please don't put in that I told you.

I bet Marty had some trip, I was very sorry to hear about her hand, with my football, we have a lot in common, I have a sneaking suspicion I have written this before.

Give every one my Love, Mouse

BLAME IT ON THE DICTAPHONE

To PH, October 7, 1942
Finca Vigía, Cuba

Dearest Mousie:

We were awfully glad to get your letter and to hear that you were such a good football player and that school was as good as you had expected. Gigi wrote you about poor Bates dying. It was really awful. He had the same thing that killed Pony, that took so long for him to die, but we gave him all the medicine he should have had and took good care of him and did everything that we could about it. But Gigi felt awful about it and we didn't know how he would stand up under it finally. He took it very well really because he has such good sense and though he loved Bates he knew there was nothing we could do about it. The other thing that helped him out is that Wolfer has got to be such a fine cat and that we have Testor's new baby who is a wonder cat.

Gigi plays with his ball team and is really pitching very well. It was a big blow to him to have the Yankees beaten by the Cardinals the way they were and he lost fifteen bucks on the series. He went with Mayito to the Pan American the first day to hear it and the second day went with Juan to the big score board in the park. After that he went with me to listen to it here at the house and we heard it very well on the radio here and kept score. The last game we heard down in the cove on the boat radio and it was a bitter blow to the old man.

Boysy is in fine shape and so is Willy and so is the new cat and Stooppy Wolfer. I found that what was the matter with your catnip was that you planted it too shallow. You needed to drill down the holes and plant it deep because what was coming up as long stalks with you was really the roots of the plant. Once you planted it deep enough the leaves had a chance to develop.

Marty is coming up to New York and will be there on the eleventh. She and Wolfer will come out to see you at school if it is possible. If she can't make it out to the school she'll talk to you on the telephone. Anyway, you'll get a chance to get out to Gardner's Island and shoot there over Thanksgiving holidays. I'll fix it up with Wolfer when he is down here exactly how you are to do that.

If this letter is jerky and doesn't seem to make too good sense, blame it on the dictaphone which Papa is trying out for the first time. It shows at least that we are getting somewhere to have a dictaphone anyway. Its lovely at the finca now and we all certainly miss you and wish you were here. There are plenty of quail in the back country. Every time Marty or Gigi go out they run into at least a couple of big coveys. Gigi hasn't gone out on any big dove shoots or quail shoots yet but he has won about fifty bucks in team shoots and [HANDWRITTEN: miss and outs.] He still is about $65 ahead even with his World Series losses.

There're lots of birds coming through now all sorts of warblers, crioles, and small birds that I haven't had time to identify. There are also big flights of teal coming across which probably means an early winter.

All the scientific projects are in fine shape and everything will be okay with them. Dearest Mousie we miss you very much, both as a brother, a partner and a [HANDWRITTEN: joke] companion. It isn't the same here without you at all. I'm going to have Marty get the seats on the plane for you for the day after Christmas, so that you will be sure to have them and there will be no excuse for you not getting down here. They have almost finished the picture of, "For Whom the Bell Tolls" and talk about sending it to New York and having me come up to see it. I will try and get them to send it down here so we'll have a look at it. Cooper and Bergman ought to be good, no matter how the rest of them are.

Mousy, write about school and tell us all about it. We all want to know how it is. Give my love to the H. Fs. and much love to you from all of us. Much love from Papa.

[AUTOGRAPH POSTSCRIPT:] Will write often. Gigi wrote yesterday. Max Perkins is sending the big book about football always remember to swing your arms wide when you tackle. Open them wide before you make and then slam them together hard. Like slapping them together across your chest. Try always to fall sideways so to protect your balls as in boxing.

Wear a jockstrap when you play.

Papa.

FIELDGLASSES

To EH, October 11, 1942
Canterbury School

Dear Papa

I got another letter from Wolfer, he said he was leaving for Cuba on the 10, so I guess he will get there before this letter.

The first team played their opening game of our schedule, (Mr. Gibbs the English teach would kill me if he knew that I changed from the first, to the third person plural, but I know you would understand) we lost, 6 to notin', but maybe we will win the next.

Papa do you think it would be [?] alright if you sent my fieldglasses over with someone to Miami, so I could have them up here?

I need them up here quite a bit.

Mother is coming to visit me next weekend, I will be very glad to see her.

Christmas vacation is still undecided, but Mother or me will wire you as soon as we know.

I sure wish I could write you more, but there just isn't anything to say.

Love Mouse

PS Very much love for Gigi and Marty

A PLACE WE ELECT TO GO

To PH, October 15, 1942
Finca Vigía, Cuba

Dearest Mouse of Mice:

Today I got your second letter and boy were we all pleased to have it. I read it out loud to Gigi and translated it into Spanish for Don Andres who was here for lunch. Things certainly sound terrific at dear, old Canterbury.

Today I got a wire from Marty asking me to fix it up with mother to try and get the Headmaster to let you off for Saturday to go down to Gardner's Island and shoot with the Wolfman. I sent the wire right off to mother and asked her to intercede so you could have that one shoot. School seems to be principally devoted to taking the vacations away from men as far as I can see so far. Your handwriting has gone to hell, you spell much worse, but thank God you can still make a job. I certainly hope that they let you off for that trip to go down and shoot over this week end since there is not going to be any Thanksgiving vacation. If they don't, you can rely on Papa to throw the full weight of the Hemingstein fortune, rhetoric, and will to victory against school from now on. One of the reasons I was induced to accept school was on account of these long vacations; remember those long vacations? After all school is not kept by the federal government or by any state government; it's a place that we elect to go to. On the other hand, remember that any school seems difficult at the start and they are all cut out of much the same cloth. It isn't like the old home study, literary society, and self improvement organizations that we run at the finca. It's School, and one thing we learn in this world is that you have to eat a ton of it, and you might as well start now with school. The Head master's own boy ended up a rummy, and at least we can set a good example by none of us becoming rummies, at any rate.

The above will soon produce results in case they do have censorship. But this won't get to you until after they will either have agreed to let you go on the trip to Gardner's Island or have refused it. Are there any good guys? There must be some. The black duck King sounds wonderful. He reminds me of the twelve goal polo man in the camp out West. I know how you feel about French. I never could learn any of those languages with a grammar either. But you have to swat hard at it and do as well as you can, and all of a sudden it seems to make sense. It's a shame you can't slip a couple of cog somehow and get back in your hand the time when you could only speak French when I picked you up at Bourdeaux that time and you couldn't understand English at all. Grammar always seems dopey when you study it; but in the end it really makes awfully good sense. But French grammar is as irritating as any of them. It'll be good for your old bean to work it through though. We have to work out all we're weak in to always compensate what we are strong on.

Has the big airplane book come from Mac's yet? If it hasn't, let me know and I'll keep after him about sending it. Will also look up some other good books and fire them on to you. I know that funny book must pall in the end.

Gigi has taken his mob over to play this afternoon at the Glub de Casadores. There they will make their first experience with the grounder that doesn't have to hit a rock or that cement pillar before it bounces. Let's hope they'll like the grounder when they actually meet it. Since Enos Slaughter and Terry Moore were so terrific for the Cardinal in the World Series, Gigi has spells of thinking he would like to be an outfielder; his only trouble is catching the batted ball. If he could only learn to catch flies, he could probably be one of the greatest out fielders of all times. He certainly knows all the statistics.

Gee, Mousy, I hope they fix it up so you can make that shoot out at Gardner's Island. If they don't I'm going to get kind of rabid because I was induced to accept the place on the grounds of long vacations, and since we have already been gypped on the starting time and nobody yet know about Christmas, I certainly think you ought to have that one week end. I will write airmail to the management and find out about Christmas vacation. In the meantime, am getting reservations for you guys over here to Cuba for the day after Christmas. Bumby can come then too if he is free.

Work very hard at your studies because that is the only reason to put in time at school anyhow. They say school and college is where you meet the wonderful friends that accompany you through life; we know some pretty good guys in the outside world already. Though what you should do is work like hell and learn all you can and buckle down on the French, and when you don't understand things, don't be afraid to ask and have it made clear to you. I've never understood English grammar yet; the rules of it that is, and you really, truly learn a language by ear. Work as hard as you can to learn it the other way if it is possible.

I love you very much and so does Gigi and everybody here sends you their very best. Kisses from papa and Gigi.

A CREDIT TO THE FINCA

To PH, October 20, 1942
Finca Vigía, Cuba

Dearest Mousie:

Marty called me on the phone on Sunday and told me how that
Prince of Princes Dr. Hume has refused permission for you to go out
to shoot at Gardiner's Island with Winston Guest. If you can get a
good rubbing from the Head's chair showing the size of derrier I will
know what size iron re inforced boot to wear when I call on the good
doctor to pay my respects. Seriously am damned sore about it; first
the gypping on saying there were the long vacations to induce me to
consent to the school; then cancellation of Thanksgiving Vacation;
then this refusal because of it "breaking eighteen years of tradition
and besides being so good for Patrick not to go there." Will write
about Xmas to the Dr. after talk to Marty.

Mousie [Giggy] goes back on Friday the 23rd. The reason for
his return is so Ada won't have an extra trip up to Miami to meet
him. She is going down to get Key West in Shape. I had arranged,
as ordered, or requested for him to leave on the 31st. None of these
things increase my respect for the way things are managed. As a
matter of fact am becoming damned sick of them.

Here there is not much news to write. Plenty of the other kind.
Have never been working harder. All work goes very well.

DEAR PAPA

How is football? Has anyone asked my permission whether you can play football? Will have to look into that I suppose the dopes think on account Mother entered you in school I have nothing to say. Giggy has been playing lots of baseball. The other day I pitched for one team and Cucu Kohly for the other. Giggy played on mine and we won 24 26. I had the bags loaded in the ninth and had to strike out three men (you know the size men) Sunday Giggy pitched for one team with Bob Joyce on his side and beat the bunch I twirled for 22 24. Giggy's team scored 24 runs and three hits. Our glorious nine made 22 errors, never caught a flyball, except two pop ups to papa and dropped every throw to bases. Joyce can hit however. He hits plenty. He played for Giggy.

The Cats are all well. Young Thruster can climb up on the bed and make a roaring purr purr.

Pigeons have all moulted and have new feathers and are really beautiful. No more illness since several weeks.

Been no shoots since I wrote you. Giggy is going to write about what life we have had on the ocean wave.

Goodbye dearest Mousie. We all miss you so much. Make the best of school that you can. All those snot schools are that way; but naturally the ones with eighteen long years of tradition have to be the most careful of their traditions. It was in the year that their great tradition commenced that Papa was in Pamplona getting the material for The Sun Also Rises whatever the connection may be or there is none.

Shevlin sends his love, so do all your other friends and Giggy and Papa. I know you will be the fine straight boy you always are and a credit to the Finca.

Papa
Ernest Hemingway

THANKSGIVING AFTER ALL

To EH, October 22, 1942
Canterbury School

Dear Papa,

I hope you have not written the Headmaster a fiery letter yet, as he has changed his mind, and we are going to have a thanksgiving vacation after all, so I may make Gardners Island, Wolfman is coming to see me at school this weekend, and I will talk it over with him.

Mother came up to visit me last Sun day and we had a very good time together.

Marty called me up yesterday, she said she was leaving for Havana on Saturday, so she will probably get there before this letter.

We had a terrific all around case of diarea (misspelled) at school it was very funny at mass in the morning, to watch them drop like flies, Heh! Heh! but not so funny when I got it about noon.

We are having a retreat now, some fun, no classes but plenty of prayers and meditations, I have found that the main subject for meditation, is the Chicago Bairs, Joke.

I have got two fine, well written letters from Bumby! he said he had written you, so you have got it already, I am sending them on as they are also written to Gigi, he is doing a lot of shooting and no fishing, what a change.

Tomorrow the midgets have their first game, I will write you the sad news in my next letter.

Max hasn't sent the big book yet, but I guess it will come soon.

I wish there was more to say, but as I said before, very little happens here.

Give love to everybody.

Love Mouse

P.S. how is the rolifex, I miss it very much up here. I am trying to improve my writing.

GARDINERS ISLAND AT LAST

To EH, November 29, 1942
Canterbury School

Dear Papa,

I got back from Gardener's Island yesterday, I had a wonderful
time. I arrive in East Hampton on Wednesday night, but it was
too rough to cross to the Island. We went over on early Friday
morning. We spent the morning in a duck blind, boy those black
are smart! They came in all right, only about seventy yards out, it
seemed they knew just how near they could get before they were in
range. We finally shot two, I got one, and the boy who was with me,
Charles Clark, got the other. They certainly are a fine duck.

On the way back we saw six geese come in to Home Pond, they
came right to where they feed the tame geese and ducks, so Jimmy
Eckles drove us up to the sand bar that runs across the mouth of
the Pond. The three of us, Mr. Neal, who was also staying at the
Island, Charles Clarke, and my self stationed ourselves along the
bar, and Mr. Eckles went to scare them over us, they came over us,
only just too far over too the left of us, I was to the only one who
had a shot, I was so excited seeing those huge animals I missed my
shot completely. It was wonderful seeing them just the same.

Just before lunch we went after Pheasants, we got seven in
about ten minutes, I got five, Clarke got one, and Mr. Eckles got
one, it was wonderful to see those grand old birds again.

We had a wonderful Thanksgiving dinner, a big turkey.

After dinner, we went after deer I missed a swell shot on a nice buck, about 170 yards, I forgot all about squeezing off, I shot over about three yards, it was very imberesink, as you readly imagine. Clark shot on any way, it was a doe, but we were getting pretty desperate by that time.

After we hunted the deer, we went after black duck again, it was just light enough to see them, they were coming in to bed up for the night, we had some wonderful shooting for about ten minutes.

By the time we got back it was dark, so that ended the shooting.

Everyone was wonderful to us on the Island. We had a very good time.

We had to get up at five the next morning in order to make the train for New York.

We had diner in New York and then took the train for school.

I hope you got my letter telling about Xmas vacation, I will let you know by wire off any new arrangements, as it is I will probably get out on the fifteenth of December, I have written Mother this, and school has probably wrote her to, I guess she will wright you about it.

I am know playing basket ball, I am not much good at it, and what is worse is that I don't care for it at all, I can hardly wait till we play baseball in the spring.

I miss you very much, but it is only two more weeks till Xmas vacation and we will all be together.

Love Mouse

P.S. Please give love to Marty and Wolfer and Mr. Shevlin.
(Miss spelled)

DRUNKEN SOLDIER

To EH, January 10, 1943
Canterbury School

Dear Papa,

I had a fine trip up here everything turned out good, the rail road tickets were at the Miami Colonial when I got there, Mother received the telegram the same day you sent it.

The new Duck Book was here when I got back to school, it certainly is a fine book. Thank you very much.

School is just the same, we have mid year exams beginning on Saturday, I hope I get good marks, anyhow I am working very hard.

The weather is very clear and cold, it goes to 10 above every night, it certainly is a change from Cuba.

I talked to Mother in Miami she sounded fine, everyone seems to be fine in Key West.

The train I came up on was not crowded but there were a lot of soldiers. There was one who was quite drunk he kept me awake for quite awhile until he finally went to sleep.

I sorry this is soo short but I can't seem to concentrate with the "Family Prayer Period" going full blast on the radio and the boys pounding on the table.

Please give my love to Wolfer and Shevelink and the boys.

Love Mouse

P.S. The doctor said there was nothing wrong with me. I feel good.

A LETTER TO CHEER HIM UP

To EH, April 4, 1943
Canterbury School

Dear Papa,

Here I am back at good, old school. I had a very uneventful trip. The plane trip to Miami was very rough and it was only luck that I did not get sick.

Mother and Gigi were in Miami to meet me. We had one day together before my train left for New York. Gigi seemed very well but gloomy about going back to school. I think he would like a letter to cheer him up.

I had a very wonderful trip up by train. The scenery was so beautiful, I was in such wonderful joy.

The train, "The Silver Meteor" was three hours late. Wonderful speed!

School is very cold, but hundreds of Robins on the grounds give hope for better and I hope warmer days.

I have to stop now to study History as I have very much of it, and very little time to do it in.

Please give love to Marty, Wolfer, Don, Pache, Gregorio Ternandeull, the cats, ect, ect.

Much love
Mouse

Patrick Hemingway

MISSED YOU WHEN YOU WENT

To PH, August 9, 1943
Finca Vigía, Cuba

Dearest Mouse:

Certainly missed you when you went! Been very busy with
boat and all also training hard to be in good shape for shoot.
Won Sunday shoot with a 25 17 of them were hard and about 3
impossibles. Even had the public in our favour finally. Worst frye
you ever saw by Grobiel. Must have cost at least $1200. Had to get
rid of 8 shooters in the shoot off. All cats fine. Marty fine. Gigi fine.
Do you remember Floradella? An old guy named Copin who hadn't
shot since 1937 won the trap championship with 100 straight
almost precipitating a wave of suicides in the class shooters 2nd
100 straight in 30 years. Nuwgo 2nd Frankie 3rd with 97 and 96
Jos Maria only got an 88 am going to try to win championship.
Wish the devil you were here to shoot it with much love Papa

Willie sends his love too.

Papa

AS FUNNY AS EVER

To EH, August 21, 1943
Canterbury School

Dear Papa and Marty,

I was very glad to hear of Gigi's wonderful shooting in the championship. It was very tough luck that Fatty had globos when Gigi's were so hard.

Key West has changed even more then it had at Xmas time. The Naval Station has expanded all the way to the way to the county court house, and has wiped out almost half of colored town. There are more planes than I have ever seen anywhere else. They fly over our house all day long, and make a terrific amount of noise. The northern end of town has changed also, especially the county road which is filled with housing projects for defence workers.

Everyone we know are fine and send you their love. Mr. Thomson told me to tell you that the reason that he did not send you the net you wanted was that there was so little time until the boat left, that he was unable to find one before it left.

Gigi and I went fishing today, but we did not get anything. We used crawfish for bait, and you know how hard it is to hook gray snappers with it, as it pull of as soon as the snapper takes it in his mouth.

Gigi and I are going up to see Bumby on the twenty eighth as you suggested. It is a shame he will be there for much a shorter time, but it will be better than not seein him at all. I don't think he likes Miami very much.

I have to go to bed now, and I can think of nothing more to write.

Love Mouse

TRYING FOR THE JUNIOR TEAM

To EH, October 3, 1943
Canterbury School

Dear Papa,

I am very sorry that I did not write sooner. The first few weeks in school are such a muck, that when I get some free time I am just too lazy. I promise I will do better from now on.

The country is very nice now that the leaves are turning. It is a cold clear day today and with all the different colors it would be swell, if I were not in school.

This year I am trying to make the junior team but so far we have no coach so that I do not know how many games we will have. I am trying out for tackle, and I would be very good except for two minor details, tackling and blocking.

We have a very funny math teacher this year. He is one of those people who can't resist telling every body about his life. You know how his roommate in college was a brilliant writer and wrote an unpublished novel, but drank himself to death. All the other masters are the same as last year except that Mr. Jenkins the rummy Spanish teacher did not come back. Please write me about that fishing on the trip.

Love
Mouse

BACK ON THE MIDGETS

To EH, October 14, 1943 (age 15)
Canterbury School

Dear Papa,

I am sorry about the handwriting. I think that it is laziness more than anything. I will try and do better from now on. It is a shame that the long trip has been held up. Remember how last Xmas we kept waiting for the Norther that never came? Maybe it will be like that this year, and the fish will not sound because of the cold.

I have been kicked off the junior team because I am too light, so I am back on the midgets. Anyway I will at least make first string. Just before I got kicked off, day before yesterday, I got a knee in the teeth while I was tackling. It loosened my right front tooth so that I could wiggle it back and forth, but it is a lot better now, although it is still loose. I think that it will harden back in place.

We have been having swell fall weather this last week. It is just made for pheasant shooting. I hope you get to come up here so we can do some. It has not been really cold enough to send the ducks down yet. But it's bound to be on the way.

I do not have Bumbies address nor have I heard from him, but I will get it from mother and write him. Maybe he will write me back. I guess he is having a pretty busy time right now and so is not writing.

I have been having a pretty tough time with my lessons the last two weeks. My math is still my weakest subject. I just squeaked through with a sixty on my last test. It was on factoring and, for me anyway, quite hard. I am well off for books for this term anyway. I went to Scribnirs with Marty on my way up and I got some then.

I have received two very nice letters from Gigi. Aunt Jenny sent him, and me too, a canvas boat from abc & Fitch that we can use to go fishing up on the keys, as it can be folded and put in a car.

Last week, maybe I have told you this before, a deer came right up on the school lawn during lunch time, and although it was only a doe it was pretty good for this worn out country. That is all the game I have seen here this year so far, not even a pheasant has been here.

It gets pretty dull up here and if I did not have to work all the time, I would really get sick of it.

Please give love to Wolfer, Gregorio, Patche, Dini and all.

Love
Mouse

A BIG DAY FOR FOOTBALL

To EH, October 28, 1943
Canterbury School

Dear Papa,

I have not heard from you so I take it you have started the big trip. Boy! I wish I were there. I hope you take plenty of pictures so that I can see what it was like when you come back.

I have had a pretty good time this week. The five week marking period is almost over and therefore the work has not been so hard, even though I have had lots of tests. I ought to get pretty good marks this period. All my marks except math are eighty or better, and even it is not so bad, but I never can tell. This next week may be extra hard.

Saturday was a big day for a football. All three teams had games, either here or away. I am still on the third team this year. Our game was at South Kent. We went there by train in the morning, ate lunch, and played the game in the afternoon. We won 20 to nothing. The third team, and the second team won their games, but the first team lost 6 to nothing.

Is there any chance that you will be up here at Thanksgiving? I certainly hope so. We could have very good time.

Much love to Wolfer and the boys, also Don Andres.

Love
Mouse

LONESOMER THAN LIMBO

To PH, October 30, 1943
Finca Vigía, Cuba

Dearest Moose:

Glad to get your letter and know that the glorious old third team is still rolling them in the alleys. The hell with the other two teams. Me for the third. I hope you set fire to the town after the victory. Evidently you are carrying on the great pig skin traditions of Papa who was known as Droopy Drawers the Sagging All American and Bumby who was called The Spavined Mule of the Hudson in his great days not to mention your Grandfather who could run both ways with equal ease when carrying the ball and always had to be accompanied by a man with a Compass to tell him which goal line to cross. He was the Greatest Erratic Full Back ever to play in the middle west. No one ever knew whether he would produce a touchdown or a safety when he seized the ball (usually on the wrong signal).

The Marty got away last Monday for her destination. Bumby's also evidently over. Great quantities of ducks have come down with the cold wave there's been in Miami and thousands of snipe. We hope get away Tuesday for a while but not where we thought. No fish there now.

BOARDING SCHOOL

Will you find out about vacation? The dates I mean. And
let me know so can plan to be here. Looks like going north in
November is out for me because we have had such a long delay.
It was really an awful month. Until the last three days not a good
day and right now a big brisote but it feels wonderful. Do you
[EH CANCELLATION: Negrita has two] remember Floradella?
No that is joke. I mean do you remember that Basque captain we
call Sinbad? Tall, that played water polo with us once? Have been
carrying him instead of Dini. Honest Don is gone too.

Old Moose I certainly miss you. It is lonesomer than Limbo
here. Only the cotsies for company. Your Will as fine as ever. Boisie
very loving and good. Friendless has gotten to be a great cat.
Thruster mean and distant. Tester nice with me but mean with
everybody else. Furhouse and Bro fine. Fots is as big as a skunk
and moves the same way. He is a fine slow friendly good cat.

Must go in town now to meet the lower element for lunch at
the Floridita and then face the ferocious correo at a distance of
25meters. Today is Sat. Always a big day at the Floridita.

Thanks for writing so often and for being so careful with the
penmanship. Much love from Papa.

E. Hemingway.

FIRST SOPHOMORE REPORT CARD

To EH, November 2, 1943
Canterbury School

Dear Papa,

My marks came out for the first five week period yesterday, and I thought you would like to see the report. It is certainly much better than last year. I hope I can keep it up and maybe do better next time. My Math and English could both come up quite a bit. I had the third highest average in my form. The first average in it was 89% and so was the second.

Is there any chance that you would come up North around Thanksgiving. If you are it would be swell. If you don't I will have to find out where to go, as we are not allowed to go to New York or anywhere else alone.

Much love to Wolfer. I will write him this week, also to the boys,

Love
Mouse

ALONE HERE AS I WRITE

To PH, November 10, 1943
Finca Vigía, Cuba

Dearest Mouse:

I was very proud of your marks. you did splendidly. Wolfer sends
his congratulations two as does everyone on board. Got your 2
letters (the first one about the skunk!) when Juan brought mail to
Bahia Honda. Send this back by Juan.

We had been out a week when the norther hit. I can't get up for
Thanksgiving I am afraid but Wolfer will be and he will call you
at school and do whatever is necessary to get you down so you can
have a shoot and some fun.

It is so cold I have on two sweaters and a coat writing in the
cockpit. Yesterday we saved Thorwald's shark schooner which had
broken her moorings and was drifting onto the rocks with no one
aboard. If it hadn't been a friends we could have gotten salvage
Gregorio has gone in to meet Patchi, Wolfer and Sinbad who all
went into town yesterday when the big blow bottled us in here. So
I am alone here as I write.

Boy it is no day for a frozen Daiquiri more like old Taylor's hot
toddy weather.

Wolfer plans to be home on the 17th and he will call you at
school and get the dope.

Marty's address is Mrs Ernest Hemingway care of Miss Virginia Caroles, U.S. Embassy, London, England.

Got cable she arrived okay. Know she would love to hear from you.

Bet the cats are cold. You ought to see Willy come in and sleep under the sheets in a norther. If this keeps up indefinitely I'll leave Gregorio and Patxchi on board for a couple of days and go home and see them. Certainly miss my cats, my Mouse and old Gigi no use missing the Bumby or the Marty because they are too far away.

Well Mouse will be seeing you soon. Congratulations again on the fine marks. Keep it up. That's the only reason to lose all this time all of us away from each other.

Much love
Papa

GARDINERS ISLAND AGAIN

To EH, November 28, 1943
Canterbury School

Dear Papa,

I really had a wonderful time at Thanksgiving. Wolfer was not able
to be there because he had to spend the Holiday with his wife, and
mother. It was swell just the same.

I left school at noon at got to the island that night at seven
thirty. Jimmy Eckles and I started after breakfast for deer, about
seven thirty. I got seven by ten oclock. I have never seen so many
deer, almost like our old friend, the jack rabbit. The first one was
a down hill shot. He was looking back over his shoulder. I aimed
in the general direction and jerked off. To my great surprise, he
fell. I was shooting a 220 Swift, and the bullet broke his neck. I
can't remember the details of the next two, except that they were
also shot in the neck. The fourth was quite easy; we came on him
right in the middle of the road, facing us at about seventy yards.
His neck was broken too. The next two were kind of strange. We
saw a doe at about a hundred yards in the roads. Behind her, up
on a hill, was a nice buck. We stopped the car, and he walked right
towards to look at the doe and gave me a swell shot. Right after
he fell, I saw another with just his head and horns above the mist.
The bullet went under his chin, up into his brain. We got the last
one after we had taken five of them back to the house. He had

only one horn, the other must have been shot off. I got him above the shoulder, but he ran for about two hundred feet. The gun was perfect; it did not kick and shot perfectly flat.

After we went after deer, we had something to eat, and tried for pheasants. They were in that thick, thorny cover, and hard as hell to get at. I got four hens in a row, and one cock, and then missed cocks right off the bat.

We went for black ducks in the afternoon. They didn't stop, that is, they didn't start flying until just before dark. But did they come when they started! We had them down all over, that is, Jimmy Eckles did but we only picked up about eight or nine because the dog couldn't get after them in the thorns.

It certainly is a let down to come back to school after that, but they there are only two more weeks to go till Xmas vacation, and I am counting the days!

Much love to the Boys and Don Andres.

Love
Mouse

P.S. I will probably not write again as it will be so soon till vacation, and it takes ten days for letters.

BACK IN SCHOOL, PRETTY DISMAL

To EH, January 10, 1944
Canterbury School

Dear Papa,

I am back in school now and it is pretty dismal. It was too bad that the old man was sick for most of vacation but we had a good time the two days before I had to come back here. He got a ping pong set from Uncle Gus for Xmas. We played at least twelve games of ping pong the morning after he arrived. He was in good shape except that he still had a little cold. Mother is fine and thanked you very much for the Rum, and for seeing about the tiles. Ada and Jimmy were also very pleased with the money sent them by Gigi.

The second day I was in Key West a man came over in the yard and asked me to shoot a coon which had eaten two of his chickens, and which was then sleep in the tree across the street. I shoot him with the twenty two and Mother had him skinned and cleaned to eat that night. Ada cooked him in mint sauce like a rabbit. He smelled wonderful cooking but he was not so hot eating, but the sauce was very good.

Do you remember that single shot twenty two that you bought me in Cuba which I used against the Killdeer? I painted it with preservative paint, and tested it out underwater to see if it would shoot and it shot quite well. It went through one inch of wood at a foot's range, which is not very far, but plenty to kill a fish. I did not have a chance to try it out on fish because it was too cold, but I did go out once for crawfish, and it really shocked them, much better than any spear. I got ten crawfish in about half an hour and only one which I shot got away. If it works that well on fish it will revolutionize goggle fishing, as the none hole fish, such as the red snapper, the Cuda, blue runner and so forth will be very easy targets and if you hit them in the eye or gills or head they will not be able to swim away.

Mr. Sullivan took me up to big pine and no name Keys to fish, but the water was still cold and muddy from the last Norther and all we caught were some very small grunts and schoolmasters. I took a twenty two along but we did not see anything.

I almost did not catch the bus to Miami. It was so crowded that I had to sit on the floor. The train was not crowded at all, in fact, there was a whole car empty.

The weather cold as ever. There is about two inches of packed snow, and the temperature was down to 0 degrees last night. We get up at seven in the morning, and it is completely dark.

I missed two days of school as Mother was unable to get reservations on the fourth. This broke my heart.

Have you heard anything from Bumby? When I got back there was a postcard which was dated December 4 from him but there was very little written on it.

My handwriting is starting to go and I have run out of news, so I will stop. Please write if you have time, Much Love Mouse

A BEAUTIFUL PILOT

To EH, February 4, 1944
Canterbury School

Dear Papa,

Just about ten minutes ago a Grumman Hellcat came over the school at about three hundred feet, banked off, climbed and started to stunt. Next it did a loop, then it flew, gained a little altitude, and came at us doing barrel roles. He did nine perfect ones right in a row, like a corkscrew, without losing more than a couple of hundred feet. I don't know who he was, or why he was doing all this for our benefit, but he was a beautiful pilot.

A great scene took place in English Class this morning. Somebody in the back row had a package of b.b.s and he let all fifty of them drop, one by one. About number 47, the master was pretty sore and gave us all an f for week unless the person who was dropping them would admit it. Nobody admitted it, so I guess I have an f. for this week.

The results of the mid years and the five week marking period came out this Monday so I am getting a 95% in Math, I managed to make a 90% average for the half year.

Grandfather has been very sick the last two weeks, and mother went up to Piggott. He never regained consciousness, and died last Thursday. I knew nothing about it until today.

Love

Mouse

P.S. Will write better next time

A STRANGE COUNTRY (ENGLAND)

To PH and Gregory, May 25, 1944
London, England

Dear Mouse and Gigi:

Well citizens this is a strange country but I like it more than any other I have ever been in except France and if it were peace time and you had plenty of money it could beat a big part of France. There are large sections of this country where the saloons, which they call pubs here, are as dry as the Gobi desert due to the American troops having drunk up everything and through those sections papa just mixes a little whisky out of the old flask with water out of a canteen and hurries on. American canteens have an aluminum cup that nests over the base of the canteen and on the way to an air field, or coming back from one, you splash some whisky in this tin and pour water onto it and watch the beautiful country you drive past. It is green as a golf course in spring but even the parky country looks like wild country in the old day before there was under growth and second growth timber. It is like it was in the great hardwood forest at home when Papa was a boy.

You cannot believe how beautiful the fields and the trees are. But the country isn't broken up nor choked and you have high rolling country and pine trees and gorse we would have to drive two thousand miles north of home to see. Nobody has very much to eat but everybody eats. The worst thing is that good beer drinkers do not get the beer they are used to and whisky drinkers are really ruined. Gin they serve in lots of pubs only to ladies.

Papa lives at a hotel where they possibly make whiskey in the kitchen because it all bears the hotel's label and it is a lot better than home grown Arkansas whisky but not as good as Cuban or Key West liquor. I am awfully glad I came over though because I had only seen the English in other countries and the one that stay at home are very different. Nobody is trying to be like anyone else here now. It is hard enough to be like themselves with all the ball room bananas that goes on with the pilot less air craft and all that coming in. It shouldn't raise as much hell as it does; but it raises plenty because the people have had five years of war and this is a new thing at the end of a war with a strange noise to it that you can confuse with other noises, and so it makes everybody listen all the time. [EH AUTOGRAPH INSERTION: Sometimes there is a bang at the end and sometimes there isn't.] Actually it doesn't kill so many people when it hits but it has a lot of blast and is a big window breaker and the glass cuts people up.

I spent quite a lot of time with the boys that shoot them down so everytime I hear one or see one I think, "There is one that got by the boys." But most of the people don't realize this and feel that this is being done to them and it isn't being stopped properly. But anybody would have to be a paranoiac to think it would hit them out of a town of ten million. Still remember all the lottery tickets we bought in Cuba with hope; or anyway with the old salesmanship shoving them at us, or throwing them into the car. And we never won anything.

Out in the country you see lots of rabbits toward evening along the hedges in the side roads and you see many big hares too. They are not as big as our jack rabbits but they are a good big hare and when we are going back and forth from the air fields we see quite a few partridges too. I haven't seen a pheasant yet but maybe we have not been in the pheasant part of the country. [EH AUTOGRAPH INSERTION: I suppose now, too, they are just hatched the chicks. But maybe they are earlier here.]

The trout streams are very low and full of weed from a light winter and a long dry spring. The U.S. soldiers have treated the streams very badly. They are old streams and every trout knows where he lives and pretty nearly every fisherman knows where every trout lives. So you can see what chucking bombs into the streams would do. It kills the trout and ruins the stream and the feed. On one fine stream, the Kennet, there was a stretch of water with three [EH TYPED INSERTION: unexploded hand grenades] marked by poles stuck in the stream. It seems pretty difficult to put an unexploded hand grenade into a stream if one has pulled the pin but that is the way they were marked anyway.

They have beautiful girls in all the villages and towns and Giggy would be in a state over them. If you think Madaleine Carol is pretty I guaranty you can beat her in the lobby of this hotel any day and if you walk down the street it would break your heart. Maybe we were all in Havana so long that all natural blondes look beautiful but if you turn and look close it isn't any illusion and there are hundreds of them that look like the movie magazines only with no fake to it. Papa got so enthusiastic he started wearing his shooting glasses instead of his reading glasses to make sure it wasn't just defective vision. But it was all true with the long legs and the high chests and all.

They are very nice and do not want you to spend a lot of money, because nobody has a lot of money except bastards, and all [EH AUTOGRAPH INSERTION: the best girls] go to work in the factory in the morning. If this war should last any time, which I doubt, or start up again, which it will if we do not handle it right, then I recommend to you guys to save what money you have in order to supplement whatever your pay will be and get over here at any cost because as far as I know nobody knows what a place it is.

Mousie can meet all the leading fly tiers (Tyers) and probably, with some difficulty gain access to the British Museum where am reliably informed are various interesting items. Gigi can get himself girls that will make him forget the loveliest thing that ever strolled down Duval Street in Key West and I will give you the very soundest type of advice available at the time. By then I should have this advice fairly well organized.

How is the ranch? Have you heard anything from Cuba? I have been working quite hard and made the landing and one sort of nonsense and another since but get back to London as often as I can because it is fine here now and [LONG EH CANCELLATION] lovely to come back to. I miss the Finca and our cats and Negrita and Waxen and poor sad Lem and worthless Juan and poker faced Justo and his beautiful un married bride and think that this is the second straight year will miss the mangoes. But we have something in England that is worth the missing of a couple of years of our own life if we can hit it sometime later when we have money.

So only read with a good light over your left shoulder and take care of your eyes. Never read with your head twisted. Never read small type. If it is small type miss the lesson. Take care of your eyes truly because I haven't taken care of mine and know what it means shooting. Then we will make our money on the Continent after the war, and the various revolutions, shooting at Deauville, Monte Carlo, San Sebastian and maybe Moscou even and we will bring the [SCAN ENDS HERE]

AUTHOR IN ROAD CRASH

To EH, June 8, 1944

Key West, Florida

Dear Papa,

I have been completely worthless since vacation. Lots of things could do, but much lazing just to hang around, so please forgive lack of letter writing.

I did not get your one of the twenty fifth of May until third of June; which shows excellence of communications, but everyone said later that accident was not serious, although first reports were not good at all. Very glad it was not bad. It would be very lousy to go three thousand miles for something Juan would be very happy to do on the way to the Club.

The Colonel (Taylor) is down here now for his vacation from Sun Valley. He has a place up on Upper Madacombe where he says there are thousands of bonefish, tarpon, and snappers. He has, in fact, caught three tarpon all over eighty pounds off the bridges. He looks in wonderful shape, and is looking forward to reopening Sun Valley after War. He says it can be done in something like three months. Gigi and I, and maybe Mr. Thompson if he can leave work, are going up this Saturday to fish with him. Hope he hasn't caught many fish in Florida by the time we get there. He's probably got that old dynamite going strong.

Will write again soon.

Much love

Mouse

PAPA'S POCKET RUBENS

To PH, September 15, 1944
Battlefields of France

Dearest Mousie:

It has been about 2 months since Papa came back to France after landing on D Day on Omaha beach. Suppose you saw that piece in colliers. After that flew with R.A.F as I wrote you and then came over to France and have been with an Infantry Division ever since except for the time that commanded a French Maquis outfit (while temporarily attached from being a correspondent). That was the best time of all but can't write you about it but will have to tell you. Was under same service Bumby is in now. It is lovely story and we need never have any long dull winter evenings until you all get sick of hearing it. We entered Paris with outfit liberated The Travellers Club, The Ritz etc. and had wonderful time. I had to write a couple of pieces and try to get them passed and then rejoined Division. We went way to the North and then East and the Division has done wonderful job and have been very happy to be with them. We have had some tough times and some wonderful times.

Haven't heard from Marty since letter dated in June. Saw all her friends in Paris and she could just as well have been there and through all that wonderful advance and fight if she had not been such a Prima Donna that she would not want one week. As it is she may have made the Southern Landing in Tolick event she will have OK story. But I am sick of her Prima Donna ism. When head was all smashed and terrible headaches etc. she would not do anything for a man that we would do for a dog. I made a very great mistake on her or else she changed very much I think probably both. But mostly the latter. I hate to lose anyone who can look so lovely and who we taught to shoot and write so well. But have torn up my tickets on her and would be glad to never see her again.

Head is all cleared up. Beat the headaches (the skull was hurt etc) and got down to 202 and thin and brown and head working fine only thing bad, as I wrote you, are eyes from so much dust etc.) but they will be OK. with changed glasses.

Mouse I miss you and the Old Man and Bumby all the time and think a lot about our fine times to come. Have not heard from the old Bum since this last business started but his Colonel promised me to find out about him and I left word at the Ritz he could use my room if he turned up. We have had very hard fighting yest and today but that is to be expected and every thing goes as it should. Am writing with the noise of the counter attack going on. I can't write you details but once the campaign is over. You will be very proud of what the Division has done and I have never been happier nor had a more useful life ever. Am saving the maps and we will put them up in the trophy room.

Thought I should write you about Marty so you would know what the score is. Am completely disgusted with her attitude in Cuba, in London and have only had one letter from her since leaving London describing the beauties of Jock Whitney's garden and how lovely it was to walk through a beautiful, quiet un warlike city like Rome. Maybe she has written others and I hear Jock is a Prisoner [INSERTION: of War] But we would be prisoners several times every day if we didn't use our heads those two egg shaped glands we had all the trouble getting down. [INSERTION: Also since we've been fighting wondered why the hell had stood being bullied so long. Love: Ball room bananas.]

In Paris I only had two days semi free but saw old friends like Sylvia Beach and Picasso and had two fine walks. It cost $100 to take six people to lunch at a moderate restaurant so usually we cooked on a gas stove in room at the Ritz.

When I was in such bloody awful shape in London have to sleep flat on back with tins on each side because head would go if it turned sideways. Capa's girl Pinkie was awfully good to me and so was another fine girl named Mary Welsh. I saw her again in Paris and we had fine time. Think you would like. Have nicknamed Papa's Pocket Rubens. If gets any thinner will promote to Pocket Tintoretto. You will have to go to metropolitan museum to get the references. Very fine girl. Looked after me [INSERTION: in worst time ever had] Mouse, my boy, if we last through next 2 weeks we will have a wonderful life.

Right now have lost my Burberry rain coat, [INSERTION: (it rains all yest.)], have a battle jacket with the zipper broken held together by safety pins, wear same two shirts worn last two months, [EH INSERTION AND CANCELLATION OF INSERTION] both at once, have head cold, chest cold, trouble on both flanks, shelling the Bejesus behind, shelling the ditto ahead, counter attack on our right, what all on our left. And never felt happier Except wish had some nose drops for head cold. Am drinking some kind of strange german Schnapps and it looks like will be fine day tomorrow.

Will you pass on to Giggy any of this he is grown up enough to take and work hard be good guy (you are) and love Papa and know he loves you and will see you in N.Y. before Christmas and we will all be together. If headmaster asks tell him Papa actually Did go abroad and to various countries there.

> Best love Moose
> Papa

Write to
> E. HEMINGWAY, War Correspondent
> c/o PRO. Hq. 4th INFANTRY DIVISION
> APO4 c/o POSTMASTER N.Y.

A MAN FED ON COW

To PH, November 19, 1944
Battlefields of France

Ernest Hemingway, War Correspondent
Ernest PRD SHREF APO 757
c/o Postmaster NYC.

Dearest Mouse:

The above is latest permanent address When you get this write there once and then the next thing I'll be calling up school from N.Y. Get your passports okayed by Mrs. Shipley so we can take off for Cuba. Please ask Mother to send Gigis passport [INSERTION: to get Mrs. Shipleys ok.] and as soon as I know when can be there will give her the dates. Write me vacation dates so I can apply for PanAm passage.

Mousie I rely on you, no matter how busy, to see that the Passports are in order and write me the vacation dates. Soon as I know that and when I know my dates can get a cable relayed to Mother.

Had hoped to get back for Thanksgiving but couldn't swing it. Regret very much as we would have had a fine time together.

Couldn't cable you direct but Hank Gorell put my name in a
couple of stories last few days so [INSERTION: if you saw them in
World Telegram or NY. Post] you would know how we were doing.
We are in the middle of a terrific damned battle Mousie that I
hope will finish off the Kraut army and end the war and I cannot
leave until our phase of it is over. That is why I didn't get back
and I couldn't tell you before hand. Then I got in some trouble
accused of commanding irregular troops (allegations of various
correspondents). These allegations were proved to be false since it
would have been impossible for me to command irregular troops
since that would have been a violation of the Geneva convention. I
had explained this situation to these troops and when they insisted
on placing themselves under my command I again explained it was
impossible since it would be a violation of the Geneva convention
but that I would be glad to offer my advice and [EH CANCELLATION:
suggestion] criticism in so far as [EH CANCELLATION: I]
[EH INSERTION: they] did not violate the Geneva convention.
Anyway it came out all right.

We've had tough time Mousler. Very tough. Now tougher than
ever.

But after this one am going to drag down, get to Cuba, fix
up grounds (trees blown down by hurricane) get in good shape,
and write book have to write book. The Mart wants to stay on in
Europe. Good chance she will end up a Dutchess I mean Duchess
we don't fight anymore once I was gone she wanted back very
much But me want some straight work, not be alone and not
have to go to war to see ones wife and then have wife want to be
in different War Theatre in order that stories not compete. Going
to get me somebody who wants to stick around with me and let

me be the writer of the family. Since childies have to be in school am not going be lonely to die and not able work. Mouse big fight today in Forest. Forest about same as back of ranch in Clark's Fork. Trees as thick as thickest. Plenty big deer that trip the trip flares at night and get shot. Haven't seen any boar yet. But many hare, fox, and deer. Last OP. was in a hunting Lodge with many good heads. Lots of wild pigeon too. Don't see many other birds as in coniferous there are really only those big black cock and higher there would be ptarmigan. I haven't seen any grouse or woodcock yet. But they would spook off with all the noise. The favourite game is the cow. In the open I watch the fall of the cow with the eye of the eagle. Mark him (her rather) on the map with co ordinates and the next day we butcher out the tenderloin. Once the cow is subjected to the fire of artillery my eye never leaves her. Place the cow under the hideous ravages of bombing I never lose sight of her. Of our own, or enemy tracers, cross the landscape I look instantly to see if Cow is in their path. Today we ate the tenderloin of the tragic cow of the opening of the offensive [EH INSERTION: She had been hiding 4 days in the basement of where we live while house rocked with shelling]. I ate 5 steaks garnished by the excellent german raw onion and washed down by Brandwein and water.

Then, stomach happy, I proceeded into the forest where the ferocious Kraut did his best to do away with us. But a man fed on cow cannot lose.

Mousie cannot remember any good advice or sound maxims to send you.

Mouse excuse worthless letter. Today very busy day up in the woods awfully sorry to miss Thanksgiving But lately we've been

missing pretty much everything But we will get it all back with
interest you have the passports fixed write me vacation dates day
you get this.

> Much love Papa
> E. Hemingway.

THE DUCK-BILLED PLATYPUS

To EH, May 17, 1945 (age 16)
Canterbury School

Dear Papa,

Letter came today. Very very funny. So glad that Mary has come
and all sickness has cleared up. I wish you could get some of the
rain we are having up here. Am seriously considering [ILLEGIBLE]
hood to get some advantage from it.

School ends Saturday, June 9th, three Saturdays from today.
Now engaged in writing great, inflated to thousand five hundred
words, essay on Christian Ethics. Haven't got title yet, but think
"The Duck billed Platypus" could be fine one. I am employing
the complete mastery (except in the spelling line) taught me this
year by the English master who looks like this: [UNFLATTERING
CARICATURE] His big strong points are "The American Language"
(H.L. Menchen), "Figure of speech", and "the majority of the
authorities". His favorite simile: she stood as a pillar of ballroom
bananas amongst the alien corn.

HOPE YOU WILL LIKE MARY

To PH, May 26, 1945
Finca Vigía, Cuba

Dear Mousie:

Just got your cable that the Atlapac reel had been delivered to
Hotel Gladstone. Enclose note to Gladstone so they can give it to
you. Am afraid, though, it may be packed in one of the trunks.

Wrote Abercrombies to send you fishing tackle catalogues so
that you could get whatever we needed down here and charge to
my account. (I've paid them up by the way)

Things are all looking up and looking fine. I am sleeping good,
spit no blood, chest and kidneys o.k. Head better all the time. It
looks as though it would be a great year for fish. Maybe wrote
you this before. Caught a 305 pound marlin, a fifty five, and a
sixty pound wahoo just going out at 12.30 p.m. The big marlin bit
exactly on the solunar table. I had to fight him on a light bonito
rig; light wire. Mary is nuts about the boat and fishing and loves
the cotsies and the place. All cotsies coming along fine. They only
needed food and care. I had wire from Bumby he gets sixty days
leave and hoped be here in two weeks said he cant wait. So we will
have that old Kraut killing type with us.

Hope you will like Mary. Gregorio is nuts about her and Don
Andres and Cucu like her very much. It certainly is lovely to have
somebody around that you love instead of that death lonesome.

She is working hard to learn Spanish to take the work of the joint off of me so can be writer instead of housekeeper.

Haven't been shooting because Alvarito has no cash and I thought might as well wait for you guys. I was bored shooting there myself with all the Montalvitos etc. It is ok when we have our mob and when you and the old man come we intend to put the boots to them properly.

When you go through N.Y. if you see any good books in Scribners have them sent down.

Capeheart is working wonderfully and have some more good records. When you come down we will make another buy. If you have time in N.Y. wish you could get any good Marlene Dietrich records. The ones we have of that old Kraut are pretty chewed up.

Have had two of your pictures framed and they stand up good.

Mouse please go through this letter and make a list of the various things. I know if you have no time in N.Y. you can't do them. But you can order the tackle by catalogue.

When is school out? Have been unable to extract this info from anyone.

So long Mouse. See soon.

Much love,
Papa.

Buy any painting stuff you need. But think can get all of that here simpler.

RED HOT CHAMPAGNE BOTTLE

To EH, September 21, 1945
Canterbury School

Dear Papa

How lovely to be back. The last few days in New York were swell just the same. The Gardin fight was just a little disappointing. Joyce who looks very much like Gavalan jabbed Barkfield so fast and countered his famous right, an invention I think of the Gillette razor blade broadcaster, that Barkfield's manager refused to let him come out at the sixth, claiming he injured the right in the first round. Couldn't have done it much harm as he only used it like Felix's. Joyce is a very pretty boxer.

I must have been in good shape when left the Finca. Not sore at all in first two days of practice nothing but blocking dummy, calisthenics, and tackling practice. I'm on senior squad but do not expect to stay there as too light and not a reflex king. Catch football like red hot champagne bottle. I never see one anyway.

Please send us copy of story when its finished. We both have nothing now to read but "plane trigonometry."

Gigi will write soon, but he is having trouble with work for first few weeks.

Love to all the boys and the Lanums when they come.

Very Much Love
Mousie

BACK ON THE JUNIORS

To EH, October 15, 1945
Canterbury School

Dear Papa,

It's swell to hear that story is going ahead so swell. Please send us a copy as soon as it's finished, if you have that many copies.

Very sorry that I fell down on the letter writing. Time goes so quickly here that I'm getting to think lifers don't have such a bad fate after all.

Speaking of "Time", I have been walking on air ever since a circular letter, with a machine printed signature, came to day saying that I have been give "priority 75" on a new Time subscription.

I'm down to the Juniors in Football again. Was on the Varsity for two weeks only. The line averages about 179lbs, so am rather relieved to be back in the light weight class (Hemingstein, the fantastic Athlete).

I was in one defensive scrimmage, playing over center, and have never seen so much dirty grass in my life.

Work is not so good this year, but think I will do better as year goes along.

Wonderful that Mary has the Spanish dominated. I am having a heck of a good French course this year. Mostly reading. We are now on a book called "Monsier Grandet". He is just like Norberg Thompson.

The Juniors played first game today. We had Wooster 28 0 at the end half. Finish school was 61 0. The end I blocked out when I pulled out was certainly not much.

Very Much Love
Mouse

AFRAID IT'S A NOVEL

To PH, October 24, 1945

Finca Vigía, Cuba

Dear Moose:

Thanks for letter of Oct. 15 that came last night. Story (afraid it's a novel) now over 70 pages. Think going to be good. Fun to write anyway. Starts in Bimini probably ends in hell. Who can tell if I can't.

Place is getting so beautiful you can't believe it. Weather like loveliest Indian summer cool, clear and wonderful. Only ten days to get through now for hurricane months to be over.

No news from Wolfie. Duck season lasts till Dec.31 in N.Y.

Am going so good writing don't think should knock off even to come up for thanksgiving. Though by then who knows?

Mary coming along fine with shooting. Likes it fine and goes down to club to practice by herself.

Am ordering wonderful new records. Did I write you the small fish are getting big enough now in pool so you can see their markings? They eat everything off the bottom and the algae on the side and pool is so clear you can see as clear as crystal springs. May be the cool weather but think fish have something to do with it.

Sounds like Juniors had hell of a team. Those 61 0 games are the kind for me. Did you know we once beat Evanston 111 0 Zuppke the great Oak Park coach who went to Illinois and

developed Red Grange etc. is down here to visit Mr. Kendrigan
and stay the winter. He is 66 but has brought his housekeeper
said to be very handsome red head. Hope she keeps a good house.
Would like to have you meet him at Christmas time. Great historic
character. He coached the great Oak Park team that played from
coast to coast and scored 415 points to 7 for the season. (not
subsidized) seven of its players made all american in college. Don't
ever let them tell you there wasn't any golden age when Bart
Macomber's old men used to go to all the games with a long leather
coat on and thousand dollar bills in his pocket to bet with the other
gamblers.

Must close to off yet
Much love to you and Gig.

Papa

EXCELLENT PLAN FOR YEAR

To PH, January 9, 1946
Finca Vigía, Cuba

WU7 INTL=HAVANA 128 9 NFT=
NLT PATRICK HEMINGWAY=
CANTERBURY SCHOOL NEWMILFORDCONN=

IF YOU CAN PURSUE THE STUDIES YOU WISH TO FOLLOW
EFFECTIVELY COMMA BELIEVE ENTER UNIVERSITY
MONTANA EXCELLENT PLAN FOR YEAR AT LEAST SINCE
BOTH PRINCETON HARVARD ABSOLUTELY OVERCROWDED
WITH RETURNING STUDENTS AS PER LETTER TO YOUR
BROTHER STOP AFTERWARDS TRANSFER PRINCETON
OR HARVARD IF YOU FIND MORE EFFECTIVE CONTINUE
STUDIES THERE STOP VERY POSSIBLE YOU MAY
WANT STUDY ART SCHOOL LATER EITHER UNISTATES
OR ABROAD STOP WANT YOU HAVE BEST POSSIBLE
EDUCATION STOP DO NOT BELIEVE YOUR EDUCATION
SHOULD BE HURRIED AND BELIEVE EASTERN COLLEGES
WILL NECESSARILY AND UNAVOIDABLY MASS PRODUCE
EDUCATION FOR

[CABLE ENDS, WRITTEN PART CONTINUES]

students who have to graduate with [EH CANCELLATION: those brands] degrees [EH INSERTION: next two years from] those institutions stop much love you and Gigi from us all stop Bumby entering Montana in March

Papa

Sender: E. Hemingway,
Hotel Ambos Mundos,
Habana, Cuba

LES TRES PICOS

To EH, January 13, 1946
Canterbury School

Dear Papa, and Mary

I wired you about the college business, but with the Western Union strike in New York, you may get this letter quicker than the wire. The problem is this: I can't graduate from this hole unless I'm accepted to some college, it doesn't matter which one.

This doesn't mean I have to go there once I get out of here, nor do I have to make the application for the fall of '46. It can be for fall of '47. But I have to make some application. Do you think it would be good to make application for admission to Montana in '46 or '47, or some other good Western college like Arizona (this is supposed to be very good), or to some Eastern college like Harvard, Princeton, Amherst, St. Johns (at Annapolis) for the fall of '46, with the idea that it was tentative, and could be broken or changed.

Please write about this as soon as you can [?], and will take your advice. I would have liked to let the thing go till at least spring vacation, but the bastard says that this is impossible, and he's right, if I go to college next year. Anyway, please send advice.

We had absolutely (shall I say that word?) wonderful luck on the way up here. This is always true going back to school.

We hit Miami at about 2:30. After try about four or five hotels we finally got one for $10 at an unknown place called "Les tres picos", or somewhat like that, settled down for a good 3 hours sleep as had to be at railroad station 7:30am to try shipside on the "champion". Gig went to ticket booth, and I pretended, with little effort, to be his idiot brother. This aroused the sympathy of the ticket agent who gave us a lower berth. So we rode up in style with the boys who had unsuccessfully represented Holy Cross in the Orange Bowl. Somehow they seemed to take little interest in us. Everything was dandy till Washington, where our lower berth stopped. From Washington to New York we stood wedged between a sailor who was an ex member of a skyscraper riveting gang, who was trying to get drunk on miniture bottles of different types of liquor with great success, and a millionaire colored woman.

We got into New York the afternoon Gig went back to school. We tried to call both Shevlin and Wolfie, but couldn't get either.

School is pretty hard now, with exams coming in two weeks, but weather is quite mild, although its blowing very hard now.

We didn't have to spend the $75 on ticket, but we spent $40 of it coming up. This seems an awfully large amount to me, but I promise we were not extravagant. I'm putting the $35 left in this letter. Thinking of money did you see that both the author of "A Naturalist in Cuba" and Aunt Anny had died last week?

Spring vacation for Gigi and me begins on March 11th and ends on April 3rd, just twenty four days, and we go to Cuba first.

Would it be all right if my roomate Charlie Clarke came down with me in the Spring. He is a nice guy, smart, likes shooting and fishing (he went with me to Gardiner's Island) and would not make any noise, very polite.

Gig hopes to write.

Very Much Love
Mouse

HOTEL OF ILL FAME

To PH, January 21, 1946
Finca Vigía, Cuba

Dear Old Mouse:

Thanks for wonderful letter. Believe that hotel mentioned is one of ill fame which makes story even funnier.

Enclose copy of cable I sent and receipt showing it was sent in case you need any proof. Remember the Doctor doubted I was really going to war.

Hope this clears up the college thing. Actually the Eastern schools are so crowded dont believe anyone will get a decent education for next two or three years [EH INSERTION: They will be having to turn out the degree needers in mass production.] I think a year spent studying painting or a year just painting and a year studying painting would be of inestimable value to you if you are going to work as a naturalist on other hand if you want to go to Montana with Bumby OK. He will have good gen on Montana by the end of school as he will be there from March on.

He is fine and will write you. Dick and Marjorie were here and [EH INSERTION: she] only blessed some one once. Papas been good. No drinkly and work hard. Place coming along wonderfully all the limes loaded garden and flower gardens are lovely. Weather very good. With so much building and all in house went down and wrote on boat 20 days and worked well.

After being so happy and wonderful for over two months Mary suddenly very unhappy about we dont see enough people, not enough friends, we dont go to the gay parties Bumby goes to, nor to dances. Me tied up all the time in work so we cant travel etc. I hope so she'll feel better about everything as I love her very much and want her to be happy. I know how hard she has tried on the house and business. Since her being unhappy came on awfully suddenly maybe it will leave the same way. Hope so. Anyway don't make any reference to it when you write.

Thanks very much for returning the movies. Bumby very impressed. After that letter he and I are going to run you Man of the Year.

Best love to Gigi. Just got his letter written after Thanksgiving today. Will write he soon. Bum got 40 doves on a dove shoot with the Merkel. He is shooting it well now.

Have to close letter as Juan going into town. All cotsies fine. Shops was very sick with flue or pneumonia but we cured him and he is fine and OK. Now. Much love from all of us. Papa. Mary sends much love to you and to Gig. Mr. BUMBY AUCH

JUSTO WAS CANNED FOR PULLING A GUN

To PH and Gregory, April 13, 1946
Finca Vigía, Cuba

Dear Mouse and Gigi:

Think mother is perfectly right that is long trip down and then
up to Piggott. Will be lonesome though such a long time without
citizens. Miss you guys bad all the time.

One thing please write me about so I can write Mother that I
think of PLAN for OPERATION PRAIRIE SCHOONER.

Your replies will be treated in strictest confidence and no one
will be quoted.

How good a driver is mother? How far has she ever driven?
How much in towns? How long haul? I am sort of worried about
undertaking trip with all eggs in one automobile when so many
lousy cars with bad rubber on roads. If Mother hasn't driven
enough to be safe on such a trip want to write suggesting will hire
Bruce for same or bad thought of getting Mr. Bumby down if his
school out.

You spoke about getting driving license. Didn't know you were
driver. Driving license supposedly indicates man's proven ability
to drive. Honest to God is a long hard trip and on almost every
cross country trip that ever made if wasn't a good driver something
awful could have happened from other people (crazies) or bad cars,
or last three smashes but remember many, many times that have

avoided bad accidents by knowledge and instinctive, long driving reflexes that don't want to commit youse guys on an un good show if can be avoided. So please write me on this right away. Because want to write mother making various suggestions and don't want to make if she has gotten to be a sound and safe cross country driver.

Also would like to check on whether you can get through the passes in Park in June and have written Bumby for his dates since worthless to visit him in school if school over. Piggott to Kansas City can be lovely trip by not going through St. Louis etc.

Local news is that Justo was canned for pulling gun on chinamen during lunch. My gun. Which he ran into Mary's room to get and came out with loaded and the safety off. Was in such a state of passion that couldn't give me gun. So had to take it away from he. Very cozy. Think Justo subject to probably increasing attacks goofihood due improperly cured early rale. Will see he gets properly treated but can't work here while such dramatic protagonist. Reasoned figured he was goofy was ate 6 chops for breakfast and was busily eating grape fruit when incident arose. Criticized by oriental he placed hand in pocket and covered slant eyed opponent from pocket as in cinema. Chiang's paisano then seized enormous knife to out the dark spot. Shouts arose (we were near dessert). Justo raced through dining room to obtain legitimate gun from beside bed. Appeared with same. Refused to relinquish due to sacred duty annihilate slant eyed opponent who had vast store of food hidden in basement. Was disarmed. Spoke to gently and advised return when calm. Returned in heavy tears. I repressed mine and tendered check for wages and told him couldn't permit even Jorge Washington to do such as had did in spite of love and respect for father of country. Now training Rene and Fico.

Doing o.k. Justo is hoping I will get him a job in the Embassy. Possibly as adviser on Chinese Relations.

Had a nice letter from Mr. Rogers that Sun Valley wouldn't be opened until winter but he was sure we would come out anyway and I am sure he will be able to fix us up someway and it will be fun. We will work something out. Pappy wrote along same lines.

Thank Charley very much for Mary and me for his letter.

Hope everything is going well and I know you are having to work awfully hard and hate to ask you to write but would like to have answers to all the questions in this rambling letter. Ask Gig to write too because not writing at all is a bad habit to get in. It can get to be a habit and then I never hear at all.

[LETTER IS AUTOGRAPH FROM THIS POINT FORWARD:]

Mary sends much love. papa auch Papa.

Wrote nearly 4,000 last week. am in a good funny part.

PROUD TO HAVE SUCH BRAINY BOYS

To PH and Gregory, May 16, 1946
Finca Vigía, Cuba

Dear Mouse and Gigi:

Glad to get letter Moose and will look after the bags. Could only
locate one bag and have Mary looking now and will give you gen at
end of this letter.

Have ordered big lot of books again to upbuild back log.
Ballet Russe of Monte Carlo been here this week. Mary and I
went on Tues. (very good) She went last night with Joy and we
are going again on Friday. Been going good on book. Way over
700 now. Worked sun, mon, tues, wed, now today laying off this
morning to write you and Bum and send some necessary wires.
Have terrific bottle neck of unanswered letters. This summer,
when you don't have school, let's keep in close touch so as not to
get balled up on the summer. Want Gig to write too. Haven't had
letter since went to Canterbury I think. Know what a devil of a
job school is. But getting in habit of never writing at all is bad
habit when school takes major part of citizens time and old mon
see very little.

Good luck in your finals. Maps fine idea. Map making also.
Differentiate Kiss baffles me. Feel like old Italian woman proud
to have such brainy boys who can read and write. Every day I try
to get a little more grammar into book so my children will not

laugh at me. They laughed at him until he addressed the waiter in Sanscrit.

Does Dr. Hume want me to come up to address graduating Class on The Life of The Spirit In Wartime?

So long citizens. When does mother plan to leave Key West for Piggott? Need for sending robes.

Much love to youse both.

Mary sends much love.

Papa

Mother leaves. wrote to him about gen on when his college out, whether he would drive, his estimate of mother's driving capabilities. It gets discouraging. Wrote him same day as did you. Seems like all he can lift a pen to do is endorse checks. It is only when the endorsed checks come in that I know whether he has received a letter no matter how urgent the subject is I write him on. Am getting fed.

I EXPECT YOU THREE TO WRITE

To PH, June 21, 1946
Finca Vigía, Cuba

FINCA VIGÍA,
SAN FRANCISCO DE PAULA, CUBA

Dear Mouse:

Please get a load of this and ring it up in the cash register however you will.

I know you had big graduationie; trip to Piggott; impending draft; visit of Aunt Jinny etc. Understand all and am not a good letter writer myself: But we are more or less the same kind of letter writer: conscientious in the clutch and cheerful if there is any cheer to be dredged up.

On letters I have been appealing to Bum for a long time. It has had quite worthless results. He never answered me about his baggage (in N.Y.) much of it mine. Wrote him 3 letters on this. He never wrote his mother after March. (She has just cabled me) I have no addresses for any of you for the next three weeks if anything comes up.

I wrote you to school to please give me all the dope and to keep in close touch. Have heard nothing since appeal for finding sleeping bags. Have not heard how you nor Giggy did; what marks; nothing.

Received a letter from Giggy today with seven mistakes in spelling telling me you would be at a certain address in Hollywood by July 15; that you were all leaving immediately and with a competent summary of possible route. Nothing about when I should expect you to be free nor any information that might help in planning a trip.

It is very possible I will hear from you and get some information on travelling conditions (invaluable gen) and your plans. Had hoped to have this now to make my own plans. But bloody what all nothing. It is really and truly disgusting.

Some sort of measures have to be taken about this business. Evidently Bumby only respects military discipline (while in Army) and you and Giggy only respect school and religious discipline. So there is going to have to be some discipline. [EH AUTOGRAPH INSERTION: There will be.]

I wish to hear from you and Giggy and Bumby on the first and the fifteenth of each month throughout the year. The letters are not to be hurried, nor sullen, nor forced; but are to be as good letters as you can write at bi monthly intervals. These letters will total 24 a year.

If I do not receive these letters for any other reason than illness on your part I will immediately take the steps which will outline to you in a further letter. I expect you three to write on the first and fifteenth of each month after you have received this letter and circulated it to Bumby and Giggy for their signatures. The last one initialing or signing it will return it to me.

I am truly very serious about this my dear and good and well loved brother Mouse and am going to go through with it if it means cutting my hand off. Bumby and Giggy have gotten rotten sloppy about keeping contact and you have gotten infected with it.

Much love Papa.

[. . .]

June 30

Have never heard what rods you took nor anything about tackle. If my rods repaired, whether with you or what.

I know it is dopy to do but I worry like a bastard about this trip on acct. of conditions being what they are and me having all my eggs in the one basket. Wake in the night and worry and think surely will hear in morning mail. Nothing in morning mail. Think well will certainly hear in evening mail. Nothing in evening mail. Been 13 days since you shoved off and ni le post card. Think very careless of all four; or else bad lack of imagination. Knocks the hell out of my working. Keep plugging at same but worry is just like carrying extra weight.

Is probably remembering the accnidlies of past two years, every one of them nobodies fault, that give me the worries. Don't believe it is getting yellow like Gen B. But if he had all three regiments committed and heard absolutely nothing; nor got any gen he needed to operate on believe even Lost Leader would be justified in le worry.

Isn't as though had not written you, Bum and mother was worried about trip and to please keep in touch.

Around page 900 on book mss. Don't know exactly on acct. so many insert pages.

When you write please send exact dates when you have to leave Sun Valley (or rather when you have to be at school and college) so I can have something to work on. Also let me know about all things which mention in this letter and about which have not heard.

The letter situation really has to be reformed as you can see with a slight examination of conscience.

Hope you've had wonderful trip. Please write me all gen that will be useful to us.

Mary sends much love.

Best love to all.

Papa

That letter of June 21 (enclosed) is in force. Instead of the 1st and 15th of every month you can write on the first and third Sunday of every month if that is more convenient and thus couple it with religious duties. But there are going to be 2 letters per month per man. So learn to like it and maybe youse will turn out to outwrite Madame de Sevigne.

EXCELLENT ACCOUNT OF TRIP

To PH and Gregory, July 23, 1946
Finca Vigía, Cuba

FINCA VIGÍA,
SAN FRANCISCO DE PAULA, CUBA

Dear Childnies:

Thanks for really fine letters giving excellent account of trip and
for the birthday cable.

Went out fishing on Birthday and caught nothing but had good
meal and swim and cake at home at night. Thought old hunch on
21st for big fish might work but the big ones just haven't come
in due to lack of current. Bruce was here for in the morning and
Roberto Herrera (El Campeon) and Roger Townsend (a P*63
fighter pilot who was down here last year and who had come down
for some fishing (there aint none) and Mary and I celebrated.
Didn't have party at club as Felix on vacation, it was a Sunday and
Don Andres had to stand by the Iglesia and Patxchi and Julian and
Guillermo in Mexico. Had a fine present of cotnip from the cotsies
and a pair of swimming trunks and some nuts in bottles or jars
(very fresh) and some good caviar from Mary and a case of wine
from Cucu and Bebo Kohly and another one from Pat. Gallaretta.
So had fine jolly day. Also a long 12 page single space letter from
Gen. Buck Lanham. Think he'll come out to shoot this fall.

Here is the gen on Sun Valley rendezvous.

Sun Valley is not yet open Mr. Rogers wired yest. but he is getting accommodations in Ketchum. (This was when he expected us from 1st to 15th.) He will doubtless have accommodations later. I cabled him today to have the accommodations for the 21st definitely and would cable him if could make it any earlier.

So it looks like this:

Am bitched by force majeur on three weeks hoped to have with you in August. Will crack down on book and try and get that much ahead. But am tired from jamming hard right up until now when expected to leave. Will get in some good work though.

You guys can stay with Mother until time to arrive Sun Valley (21st August as latest basic date) or I will finance a fishing trip of you guys and Bum if Bum wants you. Do not want to impose on him as he sounds as though did excellent job on trip and finding you fishing. Or Gig might want to stay with Mother and Mouse fish with Bum. I do not know mother's plans and do not want to upset them. So please realize that is attitude and am only putting out the Hemingstein capabilities and insert the necessary good will.

Please talk it over among yourselves and decide what is best to do with Mother and then write me

A. What you are going to do.

B. If you are making a trip how much cash you will need so I can send it.

C. Give me three addresses for the time between Aug.1 and Aug.21 where I can reach you. If you are going to be in the Sun Valley area I will write you care of Pappy Arnold, Sun Valley, Idaho.

D. Show up in Ketchum (contact Pappy Arnold) on August 21

Monies are scarce but can finance trip on same approximate

pro rata you spent for comparable time on trip from Piggott to coast. If you could cut it down would be useful. But can finance that o.k.

Enclose check for $150. for Bumby (have previously sent Mother what he owes and Mouse's and Gigi's gastos on trip from Piggott). This sent in case Bum is shoving and you not going with him so that he will not be held up.

Hope you went out to Slim's and got in touch with Coopers. Slim would feel bad if you didn't get hold of her. They have fine place.

Air mail from Los Angeles only takes 2 days now. So write me when you get this. You can certainly all write excellent letters when you decide to throw a punch. Very good. Papa pleased. Keep it up. Had been accepting bids on all of you from a prominent local glue factory (between Club and Luyano).

Could not make out completely from Mouse's letter what rods of mine you have with you. Please clarify. Mousie's gen was colorful but obscure.

Please take a pencil and mark all questions in this letter 1,2,3,4 and then answer them all. Sorry to be such a bore but stafferooing a trip under present conditions (here) without gen and trying to write book very difficult.

I want to get some really good fishing. Have had no trout fishing since 1939 and will entertain any reasonable proposition to get onto good steel head water. Especially, when we could maybe get some of the big ones. It sounds wonderful. Would like to get some of those really big rainbow in Crystal Creek with minnows all same Bum too.

And if can find name of that Col. I knew who controlled best fishing in Targhee hook up with him. Want to do a lot of shooting too because have had none at all except the miserable 8 birds at the club plus desempate. Am probably not going to live much longer and could use a fine fall. (Thus usual line: poor old papa. He won't live much longer. Somebody bring him his breakfast).

Much love to all and keep on writing. Will have to give a trophy for the Finest Letter of The Year with points for penmanship, humor, spelling, readability, and accuracy. We could call it the Madame de Sevigne Bowl.

Okayly let's hear from you guys.

Love
Papa

Mary sends love. She is in pool.

TO KEEP IN CLOSE TOUCH

To PH, July 29, 1946
Finca Vigía, Cuba

Dear Mousie:

It's very possible I'll have a fine letter from you which will make me damned sorry I had to send this. But if I do just figure this. I asked you especially to keep in close touch and told you why I was worried.

Haven't heard from you since you wrote me about sleeping bags.

Have heard no report on you, Gig and Bum's grades.

Have no way of communicating with you.

Have had no word on your college plans.

No fall dates on your or Gigi.

Have important mail for Bumby, should be forwarded at once and no address that is good until July 15. In meantime he is going to lose all his baggage (and many things of mine).

Have received no dope which would help me plan my trip and have had to make arrangements with Mr. Rogers on acct of neglections to answer official letters I forward him unless he answers at once.

FINCA VIGIA, SAN FRANCISCO DE PAULA, CUBA

September 4 1957

Dear Mouse :

Thanks very much for the ~~wonderful~~ splendid, interesting letter you
wrote from Spain .The Buho shooting must have been wonderful .
All that is so much better value than the matan mas of the
driven birds ; although that is good to do sometimes for the
practice in taking those partridges that pour over you flying
contours down the draws and the fine high ones you get occasionally .
Will send some pictures of some of that . I wish you could give me
Amadeo's address so I could go out with him if you did not mind .

The hares I thought were very easy . You just swing well with
h them and since they had no importance as hares to an ex bitzky~~xxx~~
x man they would spin over like Bitzkis . A lot of them come at the
start and toward the end of partridge drives .Did not miss one .

Gig turned up in pretty confused state at Key West .
He wanted treatment and is getting it at Miami . I talked with his
doctor again yesterday and he said he was coming along very well and
had marked improvement after the first treatment . Am handling his
hospital and Dr. bills and treatments etc.

He wanted you to send him any money Uncle Karl had sent
him to him care of J.B .Sullivan I420 Von Phister
Street ,Key West ,Florida . He was staying with Mr. Sully
in K.W.

I suppose you know about his trips back to Boston then
Back to Africa .Then back to K.W. I don't want to bother you with
any of this .But if you know anything about his true finances I
would appreciate it . He did not pay back any of the money I staked
him to go back to Africa the first time after he came out of the
Army nor the money loaned him to get a lawyer etc. Am staking him
on everything at present and it is very expensive . But it is what he
wanted and finally he has something that seems to be doing him
good . He was out fishing day before yesterday but has a
month more at least of hospital . 140 a week for Coone alone before Dr. and lawsome Bear.

His last word was that he wants to go back to Africa . I
know he should be there to collect the money he has coming in March
but it might be a good idea, for him to have a job in Miami or
K.W. in the meantime ~~when~~ he comes out to Africa . He did not
seem to me to be in shape to go on with his medical studies .
Am going on the theory the xthing is for him to get in as good shape
as possible before he does anything and not simply fly
back and forth away from his anxieties . His confusion was considerable.

His stories banal. If you have had a notice from Rice about the
Key West property enclosed is a copy of the part pertaining to
the property of a letter I just wrote him . It is self explanatory .
Gregory , while he was in K.W. waiting for his army discharge
reduced rents for tenants etc. I can't blame him for that in his condition

But it wasn't helpful.   I am sending you check for $450. of the amount
returned me for payments of taxes etc. I made so that you will
receive something from the property and it won't seem as though
fathers are gypping childrens . I spent much much more than
that and gladly and hoped it would show a good profit . If you
don't want to have it as from the property please take it with love
as a present to you and Henny .

This ix has been a bad luck year Mouse and please
forgive me for not writing . I did not want to bother you with
my bad lucks and figured you had more or less the gen on Gig .
robably much more than I had altho I wrote you what gen I
thought you needed . Didn't hear so figured you preferred not to

PART III: YOUNG ADULTHOOD

PATRICK'S ROAD through college was not a straight line: he took a gap year between high school and college but spent it recovering from a head injury. He got into Stanford and spent two happy years there. But when he changed his mind about pursuing a career in biology, and instead returned to the classics, he transferred to Harvard and graduated from there. In 1950, he married Miss Henrietta "Henny" Broyles of Baltimore.

In the period right after college, Patrick tried many things in many places before landing in a situation where he felt fulfilled and productive. First, Patrick moved to Spain to paint, but that phase of his life was cut short by the sudden and unexpected death of his mother.

Then Patrick lived in Key West while wrapping up some family affairs, during which time he figured out that he did not want to live in Key West.

From Key West, Patrick went to Piggott, Arkansas, to try out his maternal family business, farming. He decided to stick with the farming, but to do it in Africa. He then decided to make his hobby a job by becoming a professional hunting guide. Patrick arrived in that world just as it was beginning to fade, so he eventually shifted his focus from hunting to conservation at the College of African Wildlife Management, Mweka.

THE RADIATION LABORATORIES

To EH, April 12, 1948
Stanford University, California

Dear Papa,

How quickly the time has gone by since I last wrote, heh heh.
Already two weeks into spring quarter and school out on June 9th.
Vacation very short, eight days, and I spent it in San Francisco
and Berkeley. For three months people had been groaning about
the drought, power rationed, no watering of lawns, etc., and the
rain started the Friday I left. not quitting until Registration day. I
went over and saw the University of California. What an enormous
amount of concrete. The buildings all look exactly like the Key
West post office. Especially impressed by the radiation laboratories.
Even though you are not allowed to go inside them, Very moving
like the Holy Sepulchre or something. Saw Puck, who looked in
excellent shape, cheerful, and had had lunch the day before with
Philip Chi. Up until she told me about it, I did not know he was
living out here. I have his home address now, and hope to see him
next weekend.

Other great project for the week was taking a two day aptitude
test to discover my hidden talents. Given by an organization called
Human Engineering started some years ago by Harvard to compile
statistics on all different sorts of people from given professions to
try and determine the patterns of aptitude that go with success in

those professions. Seems sort of cold blooded and they say it has no application to genius (I am safe), but interesting to see how people like doctors, lawyers, and merchant chiefs do have pretty regular characteristics. Anyway, I took the tests and came out a diplomat or an editor: low structural visualization, average memory for design low accounting ability, objective personality, no musical talent, high deductive reasoning, very high vocabulary (this my only distinction. I am twenty points above average journalist, ten points above college professor, so if you need the Word . . .).

My courses very good this quarter. Comparative vertebrate anatomy which boils down to dogfish and cat. I get my cat next week. They come about fifty to a barrel, pickled in formaldehyde, and you pick out the one that you prefer. Two people to a beast, so I am carefully noting the finger dexterity of my dogfish comrades. English pretty much the same as before, a paper a week, and training in sleep resistance in class. My instructer's name Mr. Ford and I believe, though on no evidence, a fairy. He started us off in dismal fashion. "Yes, some of you may do very well at first, but they taper off at the end. You know the story of Icarus . . ." At this point, someone, hoping to get him off on a tangent so that he would forget to give the assignment said he had never heard of Icarus. It worked, and from then on they knew their man. History is the most interesting course for me now as I am on independent study, do the regular assignments but don't have to go to class, and choose a related topic to do outside regains for a written report every two weeks. Have Anarchism this week. Just finished "A Biography of Our Martyred President William McKinley", with "an Account of the Trial, Execution and Autopsy that Was Later Performed on the Assassin." Now reading book on French anarchists.

Draft question has sort of dampened my idea, but have been working on a plan to go to Europe this summer. Do you approve of this idea? $155. one way to le Harve. Ship, an old troop transport, leaves New York June 15th, takes about nine days to cross. What to do once over there I have not worked out to any extent, but I am sure there would be something. Aunt Jinny is in Torino, maybe I could get down to Italy too. I won't go into any detail because I am so tired of typing, but would like very much to know what you think of the idea?

Love to Mary and Bum and all friends very much love

(.) (.) (.) (.)

(.) (.) (.) (.)

Moose

WHAT A BUM RUBENS IS

To EH, August 25, 1948 (age 20)
Venice, Italy

Dear Papa and Mary.

We have had a lovely trip up the peninsula, have been in Venice for
about a week, and are leaving for Milan day After tomorrow. This
the prettiest place we've been in, but don't think it would be too
good to live here until you were very old, and wanted a city that
was quiet and yet full of people and things to look at. The paintings
are marvelous, but many of the best, Tintoretto especially, still in
the churches where badly hung and lighted. The boy must have
been terrific workers. In the Ducal Palace alone there are painting
covering whole walls, with the quality still maintained. Not so
many good Titians, almost all religious subjects, at which he did
not excel. Beautiful Bellini's in the gallery of the Academia. Really,
I believe painting has degenerated. People just don't have the
technical command of paint, no matter how personally talented.
The one thing I think I have learned, is what a bum Rubens is
compared to the big three here.

In contrast, there is an enormous temporary exhibit of modern
art in the Gardina. Good representative pictures of Monet, Pissaro,
Sinley, Renoir, Manet, Degas, Touluse Lautrec, Van Gogh, Gaugin,
Seurat, and nobody else there, I guess. A fifty picture Turner

Exhibit covering his whole life. He is a big and fine surprise for me, as I had never seen anything by him before except in reproduction. I think he can beat the French light men at their own game. The seascapes even better than Homer because the color in purer and more accurately seen. Beside these two solid exhibits there is the Peggy Guggenheim collection of late (and worthless Miro's), Max Ernst, Dali, and other work of doubtful permanent value. Finally, there is the pavilions of the different countries, France, Italy, United States, Austria, Poland, Belgium, etc. There is really too much to absorb in these as there are hundreds and hundreds of pictures, but seldom more than one or two by each man. Modern Italians pretty good. In the French pavilion Chagall has big show, and I liked it very much.

I am very much excited about painting again, and can hardly wait to get back and try some myself.

Italy seems very quiet, and apparent bitterness between Communists and the rest of the people. This probably just because I don't know the language and therefore don't have much first hand information. Country seems to have completely recovered from the war, more so then France. The railroads are good, and the bus lines marvelous, better than in America, with stewardesses, and bars. Things are expensive, though, much more so than France. Think it is very hard to know Italian after having been exposed to Spanish, as they are so similar, that you pick up nothing accurately by ear.

Every one here thinks there will be war with the Ruskies in a few months but think this is the pessimistic outlook.

Trip nearly over and it has been a wonderful summer. Probably should have stayed in school what with the draft and whatall, but it was worth it. Have liked every place I was in, with possible exception of Cannes this I suppose because I didn't have a million dollars.

Very much love, (.) (.) (.) (.) (.)
Mouse

TOO TECHNICAL FOR ME NOW

To EH, October 24, 1948
Stanford University

Dear Papa and Mary,

I have been back at school now for about a month, and am living
in a much better place than last year. It is within walking distance
of classes, and I have only four room mates instead of twenty like
last year. We have a clothes line, a radio, and a coco cola machine
close by, so all the creature comforts. My roommates' names are
Walt, Willy, and Smiley. The last is called Smiley because he never
smiles. I do not like any of them too much, but what the hell its
only for three years.

I went to see Bum up in San Francisco on his birthday, and he
came down to see me here at school about two weeks ago. He has
left for Washington to see if he can get his old commission back in
the Army. He looked very healthy and in good shape both times I
saw him, and I think he is making a smart move going in the Army
at the present time. I am counting on him to protect me in the next
war. Our first line of defense is Mr. Bumby.

Aunt Louise died very suddenly a couple of weeks ago, and
mother is going to take care of Uncle Gus during November and
part of December so she will be in New York until Christmas.
As It stands now, however, We will all be together in Key West

for Christmas. If not, we will perhaps go to New York. Plans are indefinite at this time.

I am working hard, and this is the last quarter which I have to take required courses. I think I will give up Biology, and try some thing un scientific. I'm sick and tired of science. I might of made a scientist in the days of the Wunder Kamer, but things have gotten too technical for me now.

I find it very difficult to write you an interesting letter, as I am really not doing anything very interesting. I am trying to learn a little bit about Greece and Rome, but finding the going pretty tough, for I have absolutely no background in the subject. Also there is an enormous amount of reading to be done. Perhaps it is not worth the effort, but it does seem one of the few branches of knowledge that just lies there waiting to be learned and to give pleasure. The names are what give me trouble, and the geography.

Would very much like to hear from you.

                    Very much love,
                    Mouse
                    (.) (.) (.) (.) (.)

LIKE BEING IN A FOREIGN COUNTRY

To EH, November 7, 1948
Stanford University

Stanford (which is the home of the football team that was beaten 49 to 0 by Army last Saturday in Yankee stadium)

Dear Papa,

What a wonderful picture letter! I feel very stale now after two months of school and very much cheered up to hear about ducks and paintings of which (a big tear of self pity) there are not much here. It is very much like being in a foreign country you must learn the ways of a different people and it is interesting, but you never lose the feeling of self consciousness. Have had this feeling about formal education ever since I left grade school in Key West. Think the system of the tutor is the best system of education and reading (never with a conscious plan or need to meet certain specifications or standards). The minute someone starts to think why and what for he is studying he's not really interested anymore. I am flunking Logic, so you can ignore the above profound speculations on the evils of analysis.

    I have really no definite dope on Bum except that he left San Francisco to go to Washington by bus by way of Saint Louis two days after his birthday. He intended to re enlist at Washington and apply for paratrooper training so as to get a definite commission in that brand of the service for he had had no formal jump training. I got a card from him mailed at a town in Nevada that he sent on his way East in which he said he would "let me know his news as it happens". This was on October 3rd and I have not heard anything more. He left me his sleeping bag and all his fishing tackle to keep for him here. He said he would probably stay with Paul Mower's son and his wife in Washington. He does not work for Ashaway anymore, but I do not think he was fired in the sense that there was any bad feeling they simply did not need the position Bum was filling because they had dropped that line of product. I did not get this from Bum himself but from Jay Allen in New York just before I came out to school. Bum had been down to see them at their place in Carmel just after he left Ashaway. For a while Bum was going to work for Mr. Allen in a salmon shipping business he is connected with up in Seattle, but this did not turn out. The Allens very much for Mr. Bum and when I came out here and saw him he looked in the best shape I had seen him since before the war. The fact that he has left both Puck and his fishing tackle and gone to Washington with just about enough money to get him there is strong indication he intended to do what he said.

I am sure you have heard from Gig by this time. Am enclosing a letter he wrote me last week which is very fine.

My news not much. Have been reading a lot on Greece (a safe topic) and working very hard on my embryology. We had our first live chick embryos today and after two months preparation it was like saying one's first mass. I take exhaustive lecture notes and type them (have seventy pages on embryology alone) and this keeps me busy. When they say back to the womb, I can tell them what its like.

Did you go to the museum of the Risorgimento in Venice?
I remember this as being a big surprise. Very interesting (I
remember a caricature of Franz Joseph with his whole face made
up of different kinds of fruit and some very fine proclamations by
the French).

Papa, it must be very nice. Please write me all about it for it
gives me more enjoyment than anything.

Very much love,
Mouse

ALL IS NOT SOMBRE

To PH and Gregory
December 14, 1948
Villa Aprile
Cortina D'Ampezzo, Italy

Dear Mouse and Gig:

Excuse me writing combined letter but have to do a lot of business. Everything is upfoo-ed with Speiser's death. Rice seems worthless and only anxious to sell properties at any bargain counter price to get his ten percent while he is in and he has taxes now snafu-ed. Mister Papa really over the barrel with my mother very ill and, of all things, her mind not so clear at 86, and me having to back Sunny to take care of her, plus handle bad operation for Sunny. Got to do those little problems this morning. But as Mother always says your father is a financial wizard. But wish I had some sonofabeesh to wizard for me today and see what HE could scrape off the bottom of the barrel. A good grade of sheet I hope for that is what a financial needs as a basic substance to blend his wizardry with.

Yet, men, all is not sombre. On Saturday, day before yest. we shot 331 ducks to six guns. Mostly widgeon, teal, a red head they have that is about 4/5 as big as a can and really goes, some pintail and mallard and a huge fat goose plus one snipe. It was fine shooting, They didn't decoy well to our blind principally due to a very fine shot called Brereton who can talk duck better than

Papa Montero. He would turn them and then they would come over fast and spooked. Or well spooked ducks coming in from being shot at outside would make a pass. You know that pass that teal make. Nothing stooled in with set wings. No hover ducks. I shot the Breda over and under that is almost like my old Browning over and under with a Holland and Holland action copied skillfully and well while the British were a hostile nation and the Scott double pigeon gun. Shot good. Bought these guns before the last bad financial luck so we have two really fine that both of you can shoot. The Breda will fit both of you. The Scott still a touch big but Boy it shoots. I killed lots of impossibles or semis stone dead; our blind killed 45 picked up with 106 shells. This man Brereton calls with his mouth only and on a basis of little love whistles; different for each species. He could bring them away from us like Papa Montero would bring down those mallards that day.

Mouse and Gig your letters have been rare but superb. Miss Mary is picture and painter mad and I look forward to those discussions on the boat where Mr. Gigi and I will receive The True Gen. Anyway it will be much more interesting than grammar because I have actually seen the pictures while have never even laid an ablative.

Speaking of laying; as whom doesn't (Now I lay me down to Sleep) I am delighted for Mr. Bum that he has broken with the $200 princess and will be able to channel his spermatozoa into something a little less chicken (one word omitted) even though that object should be the armed forces.

Have picked out two wonderful girls he can marry here if he wanted to who have ten times anything Puck had and are not B productions like Puck and would give us a few grand children from the same amount of sperm expended and not just [EH

CANCELLATION] hogs heads of old beer bottle tops. Actually there are three; one 18 1/2, one 19 one 23 all beautiful, all charming, all funny and all healthy and from fine families. They know about pictures, ballet, sailing, music, shooting, fishing, skiing.

Now Gig about Havana: You can get Elicin through the JaiAlai. Have Rene call and ask for Carlitos Rocca who can find Elicio or let you know where he is. You know Carlitos whether you remember him or not.

Ask Paco about the licenses for the guns which Lerardi should have renewed by now. In the top left hand drawer of my desk is address of that cattleman who asked us to shoot near Holguin.

Clean all guns good (well to grammarians) and see the boys are looking after them. Write me any gen I should know. Don't take any pistols out or shoot. Very tough new laws Kid Tunero writes.

Excuse me Mouse for not answering your letter properly. Mary is writing and I will. It is a beautiful sunny Venetian day and I wish I could get to the Accademia. But writing my sons and brothers and then doing le chores et el Wizardry. (Haven't thought up any yet that will still leave dough to get home. But damn well have to so will. But sure as hell would love to be doing good writing instead of having to do what have had to do since Max, Hellinger and Speiser died.)

Love to Mother and Aunt Jinny from Miss Mary. Tell Aunt Jinny I miss reading about her in the Rome paper and awfully sorry we missed her.

Love to you characters from us both. No christmas presents this year. Will make up on Bahama trip. ALSO NOW HEAR THIS: (SIREN) No checks have ever come for anybody for deposit in October. Could Mother check on this? The last checks before that were deposited in Mouse's checking acct. and Gigi's savings

acct. As of Dec. 2 your savings acct. Gig, was $6,426.02 Mouse's
was $6050.56. Gig will you please check on these dividend checks
when you go to Finca and if there see they are all forwarded to me
for indorsement. Maybe Rene held them as 2nd class mail. The
discrepancy between Gig's account and Mouse's is that since he
went to Stanford his checks have been deposited in his checking
acct. under terms of the Trust. But no checks of Oct. 15 arrived.

> Much love
> Papa
>
> And Merry Christmas To
> Everybody
>
> Papa

I BOUGHT A BAT FOR $1

To EH, May 22, 1949 (age 20)
Stanford University

Dearest Papa,

Mother wrote me that you and Mary are getting in this week, and I will try and make up for my not writing by a long letter to meet you when arrive at the finca just when you have plenty to do and don't need it.

Bumby writes he is healthy, I am more than healthy, and Gig I have not heard from for two months, so suppose he is healthy until proved otherwise. Have just gotten through the fungi and starting in on the mosses. Must admit they don't go into them very deep. I bought a bat for a dollar yesterday (Saturday) from two boys that had Just killed it in an outside corner of the dormitory. The first time I had really looked at a bat, so very interesting. They don't look very different from a shrew or a mouse. Like a fox faced shrew that had done push ups until he had the chest expansion of Paxe. But the hind legs and tail Just like other animals. Two nipples, each set way over from the midline, so that they are almost under the arm pits. Wings just like half an umbrella the way they fold up.

I should hear in the next week or so whether my transfer

application to Harvard has been accepted, and will be relieved to learn something definite either way.

Very much love,
Mouse (.) (.) (.)

[TYPED IN RED INK ON THE VERSO]

5/29/49 PS Got letter from Harvard today and have been accepted for next fall.

KNOWLEDGE OF DOUBTFUL VALUE

To PH, May 29, 1949
Finca Vigía, Cuba

Dear Mouse:

Thanks very much for the lovely letter which got here the same night we did. Glad you had such a good trip to Lower California for vacation. Hope the Harvard transfer comes through if you really want it. Also hope final exams, etc., OK. Don't work too hard in any subject you're not interested in. Passing grades are all man needs except in the things he really cares about. Too many people come out of college, I think, with impaired memories from the temporary acquisition of knowledge of doubtful value.

Our Bahama trip is working out wonderfully. Mayito is going to take the "Delicias" again so we'll be comfortable and we have the "Tin Kid" now to work over the banks with and to fish all the places it isn't worthwhile risking the "Pilar" on. You will like her very much, I think, because the motor is not temperamental the way the "Winston's" was. It is a 4 cylinder motor that runs as steady and simply as a good car motor. And she is a seaworthy and yet extremely light boat with a draft that can go anywhere.

Please give me your time of arrival here by return mail so that we will know how to handle getting you over there. We'll work it out OK, so don't worry about it. I just want to know when you're coming. Gregorio has the boat in fine shape and Rubio has overhauled both motors. It should be an awfully good trip and we'll have the luxe of Mayito's boat.

Mary will argue or exchange views on all the Venetian painters. She spent more time at the Academia and the Escuoala San Rocco than I spent at Harry's Bar or in the Duck Vine. There are lots of really nice people who want to see you this summer when you go over there. Some very good characters that you will like.

Take it easy at the end of the term and pace yourself good so as not to get too tired and if the Harvard transfer doesn't come through don't worry. Just remember that that way you won't have to live in Boston. Will not write a longer letter although I should because yours was so good. Thanks very much for having been such a good correspondent while we were in Europe. Mary and I both appreciated the letters very much.

Much love from both of us,

[LETTER NOT SIGNED]

KEY WEST IS BOOMING

To EH, January 12, 1950
Key West, Florida

Dear Papa,

Had a quiet vacation. Met Gig in Baltimore and we flew from the
Washington airport to Miami and then to Key West after about a
three hour stop over at airport which is all torn up now as they are
doing it over in more modern style with temporary result that you
can get nothing to eat nor go to the bathroom.

Key West is booming. Three or four new motels, and lots of
out of state cars. People are starting to come there as a matter
of course when they drive to Florida. Mr. Thompson said, after
hearing how bad business and taxes were from both Norberg
and Karl, that he must be the richest of the Thompsons. The last
variation on Mr. and Mrs. Chambers is apparently that Mrs.
Chambers' memory is not as good as it used to be, but at that Mr.
Camby's is excellent because he has drinking completely under
control and now reminds Mrs. Chambers of the things she has
forgotten to do, like take Penny for a walk. Penny looks very old.

You are not missing any good weather. Have been no northers
and all the time I was there it was muggy and short rains. Gig
said it was the same way over in Cuba, but had very good time
with Adriana's brother whom Nita it seems regards as some sort

of foreign chiseler and watches very carefully that he doesn't steal the silver.

Myself am not so cheerful. Have splendid system of habit and most of the accomplishments of young lady of Georgian refinement: can paint watercolors, compose in verse, discuss Literature and the Fine Arts intelligently. Unfortunately cannot dance, sing, or play a musical instrument, am twenty one and no one has asked me to marry him. What do you advise doktor, mehr Kultur?

Please tell Mary that I have decided that what makes a good picture is its being painted by a good painter (in this I am supported by Aristotle), along with a certain clever manipulation of color, line and shadow. Latest Inside dope: Goya was a fairy.

Much love,
Mouse

CAEJOTID [AN EPIC OF CATS]

[AN ORIGINAL POEM BY PATRICK, IN THE STYLE OF THE AENEID]

Come vile slut and me instruct
What the purpose or motive fell
That led our hero into Hell,
What curiosity, what to get
With the underworld to fret:
He hated mama and the clerk
Who read the funnies in the tongue
of Polsen and Warsaw, what a jerk!
As soon as he was old enough
To steal a bike and see the world
He hastened straight for the dirty wood
That round his native city stood;
There in the oil fouled marshes found
He luckily 'neath the trash a mound
And on it a branch which said in Greek:
Admit one to the Underground.
The tule stalk our hero plucked
Then pushed the door to the world below
Where six pajamed sandhogs blast
A tile lined tunnel past the grave.
On the left and on the right
Obscuring any further sight
Stood billboards with the grim advice

DEAR PAPA

That smelling badly wasn't nice
And with the heat of hell to come
He would be smart to purchase Mum.
Past this barrier stretched a lake
Where rotting shrimp an odor make
Tumbling pink in industrial scum;
Here a helltaned partycaptan stood
And promised when 'twas calmer would
Carry our hero into the land
Where every shade has a brand
Name he's proud to sign but can't,
For the inspector said: "not fair
To adulterate a tincaned pear."
As Harry waits he curious notes
This delay an attending body bloats
And listens to the prophylactic grunts:
Souls that stretch too late in death
The language of prevention.
Stacked in rows the former children, boned
For space is limited and tightly zoned
Each stamped on the thigh in blue
Await that every devil might
Have suckling pig for Xmas as a right.
It has been more than an hour
Since a boat crossed the slime
For things to get moving long high time.
"This stuff will spoil any minute now
Unless we can ship it out with the tide!"
Yelled the captan to the other side;

Back the echoing answer came:
"That to us is all the same,
For we are self sufficient here
And have no need for the stream of goods,
It was only a contract long ago
By which God tricked us to be catered so."

My lady in her best French dress
Lies upon a marble coffin lid
And not for her comfort, for she is dead,
Two pillows raise her head to the proper height
Above her breast; and at her feet's
A pug, by which the French mark faithfulness:
She gave the roebuck grace
And wings to the gull.

ALL THIS MARRIAGE BUSINESS

To EH, May 17, 1950 (age 21)
Cambridge, Massachusetts

Dear Papa,

Sorry you have had to bother with all this marriage business while
working. At least it is over now, and thanks very much for swell last
letter and check for European trip. Do you think it would be a good idea
if I used some of it to go to Rome and buy a papal patent of nobility.
Don't think I could do much better than a comites on a Holy Year, but
it would be something: an educated son (except in spelling, but this is
a noble defect) who was also a member of the grande Segneurie de la
Saingote See: pulchrissimus divissimusque comites Del denariique.

Want very much to read book in entirety. It is a truth I am
just beginning to see that things can be read and talked about
long before they are understood, and this is why not much weight
is given by smart people to the precocity of children. I have read
almost everything you have written, but find, when I reread a story,
that I had missed the point. Also, find there is a lag in me between
reading and full comprehension, which can be a day or five years.
This makes be basically respectful of the written word, hoping for
future enlightenment, but also suspicious of being tricked, or rather,
cautious. It must be hell for the critic always to make an immediate
judgement on a work, and I don't see how these judgements are
of much value. I am just beginning to catch on to poetry (the glass

eye darkly, perhaps), and the two things that helped me the most are reading Latin in the slow way which is required in scanning the verse, reciting it etc. and the criticism of Mr. Pound on poetry. For one thing, poetry is the more the realm of the iceberg than prose, and it makes sense very much the way mathematics makes sense, only with the consent and respect of the reader, but intricate, beautiful, and in the end simple, like the very complicated formulas he resented in a three demensional models. As you say, every word depends on every other word, and this has even greater possibilities in an Inflected language like Latin. Unfortunately it is dead, and German is the only language left that resembles it much from the grammatical standpoint, and it, I am told, sounds very ugly. These inflection advantages are really more useful (wide separation of things without confusion) in poetry than prose, prose, that is, that is not meant to be read outloud. Please excuse me for reciting Mr. Pound back to you, who know him much better. Just want to indicate the line of my unoriginal thought. In the end, people all think alike, but what they pay for is the mind that does the universal things quicker and at the right time. Anyone can throw, few can pitch, and then there is the decision as to what to pitch.

Weather beautiful took a long (40miles) bicycle trip on Sunday, saw Walden, which is not very impressive, but is owned by the state, and therefore has clean water, but lots of people come to swim there in the summer from Boston, and they have made a rough beach with a bulldozer to handle them all around the lake. Now studying for exams.

Love to Mary

Love
Mouse

A GOOD WEEKEND

To EH, November 6, 1950 (age 22)
Cambridge, Massachusetts

Dear Papa,

Thanks for two swell letters. They started off good week end.
Mother and Gig both came up on Saturday. Mother looked well,
but Gig looked the best I've seen him in the last two years. He had
just quit a job working a cash register, because he had to make
up mistakes out of his own pocket, commute, and with the other
deductions for social security, taxes, employee entertainment
and so forth he felt he could do better. Mother says he has a nice
place to stay in New York way down town with four or five other
guys, and he has invited us down next Saturday to celebrate his
birthday. He does not think Dianetics will last, because they did
not make a good showing on the Coast. They filled the Shriners
Auditorium in L.A., and the head, Mr. Hubbard examined a clear
patient who has run the course successfully through under a spot
light, but she got flustered and stuttered, which is not what a clear
is supposed to do.

Mother left for Key West this morning, and she is there by
now, I guess. She said Spain was better shape than she would have
thought, but that there is no light in private places in the evening
in Madrid because the power plants have parts worn out, so that
the streets are very crowded.

I think the Puerto Ricans' problem is that their rum is not as good as Cuban, and not that we have been oppressing them, don't you? Why don't we make them independent?

Henny sends love. Both happy and liked her present. Best to Gianfranco.

Much love,
Mouse

DO YOU THINK THERE WILL BE A WAR SOON?

To EH, December 10, 1950
Revere, Massachusetts

Dear Papa,

The last month here has been upset by Henny being sick and
finally losing baby last week, but she looks and feels fine now and
we are very jolly in our new place out on the water.

There is big tide as it is more or less the end of a bay, and
when it is out, the beach is almost as wide as Daytona, but not
as white. At high tide and with a wind, the ocean comes right in
on our windows. In the big gale that flooded Long Island we lost
a lot of shingles and the gate and the electricity went out about
midnight, but it was fun and you could hear the imaginary big
aeroplanes flying around all night.

I went down to see Gig last Saturday and we went to see a
wonder show they had on birds at the Natural History Museum.

Do you think there will be a war soon? It certainly looks like
a nice struggle with the Chinese and the Russians, the toughest
people, in my ignorant opinion, in the world. Luckily, I do not think
they are naturally aggressive, so that we shall only have to fight
them on their own territory. My only wish is that it is forestalled
until the end of June.

Henny asks Mary: 'what is the best way to keep a house clean?' She is having trouble in this respect.

I hope you are all well. Love to Mary. Please remember me to Gianfranco and his family.

> Much love,
> Mouse

OUT FOR HONORS

To EH, March 27, 1951
Cambridge, Massachusetts

Dear Papa,

Have only about a month and a half more of school, for I'm excused from talking final examinations in the last term of my senior year since I'm out for honors. They let you do this because of the general and oral examinations in May are as good as finals. The end result is that I am through the second week in May, and we hope to be able to leave for Spain. On beint si bien[1] ... But I think I could learn a lot copying in the Prado, where it is not so crowded as the Louvre and not as unseemly as the Metropolitan. I wrote my draft board, but have not heard from them yet. I don't think there is any chance of my being called until September, although when things thaw out in the Spring they might start calling people quicker.

Ever since Easter it has been sunny if not so warm. Very few ducks, only bay ducks like buffle head and old squaw. I get next week off for spring vacation and we are going up and try and camp out in Maine. Hope it won't be too cold. There is a little stream in Henny's abandoned farm that is supposed to have a big smelt run that you can scoop up with your hands, but I don't know if

---

1   French, roughly, for "We are so good."

this will feed us for the whole week. I hope there are some ruffed grouse. I saw some tracks. We went up for a weekend two weeks ago to locate the place, as no one had been there since 1916. It is completely overgrown, but lovely location, a point overlooking one of those salt water rivers that are really just arms of the sea near Damerisscota. A small bluff on one side of the point, and an estuary on the other side, where the supposed smelt stream comes out. It was still frozen up when we were there. The Pilar could come right up to it, but some sort of pier would have to be put in to make a boat safe.

Please write when you can, especially about Spain. Love to Finca Mary and Gianfranco. Henny sends love.

Much love,
Mouse

USED TO LIVING WITHOUT HER HUSBAND

To EH, July 22, 1951 (age 23)

Malaga, Spain

Dear Papa,

Happy Birthday! No news here except painting going ahead much better than expected. Have done 9 oils since June, but only two sucessfulls. Paint every morning from 10 to 1, but after this there is not too much to do in Malaga. In August the good corridas start, but the heat has started already. 50 c in Granada, but cooler here, because we get the sea breeze.

Hope the Korean Armistice will cause a let up on the draft, otherwise my permission expires in September and will come back Key West to take my physical.

Someone sent me a clipping that Grandmother Hemingway had died. I think she had a very happy old age, much more so than Grandmother Pfeiffer, but then she kept her mind and was more used to living without her husband.

Henny is taking arabic lessons with a real Arab, which is much better than she could get at Harvard, but it sounds like coughing and spitting to me. Much love to Mary, Gianfranco, much love.

(.) (.) (.) Mouse

TRY AND KEEP GOOD CONTACT

To PH, September 16, 1951

FINCA VIGÍA,
SAN FRANCISCO DE PAULA, CUBA

Dear Mouse:

I'm afraid you haven't been getting the letters I've written so am
making a carbon of this and will send it to your new address,
if you've moved, when Mother sends it to me. (Straighten that
sentence out with a shoe horn.) Wrote mother for yours news and
an address. But she just sent word that you had a three months
extension from the KW. board. I've written her again for the new
address if you've moved.

German publishers B. Fischer have been authorized to pay
Bumby $2400 (10,000 DRM) and I wrote him to get $500 to you.
You'll have to arrange how to transfer it. Maybe he will be able
to write a check in dollars for deposit in your K.W. bank. Maybe
there is some simpler way. Anyway you have $500. coming from
me through Bum and they wrote they are ready to pay the money.
Here is Bum's address

Capt. John H. Hemingway 01798575
Secteur Postal 50.330

Par B.P.M. 517
APO 82
New York, NY

The address is practically a letter in itself. He is US liaison
officer to the French Third Army Corps and is stationed at
Frieburg in Briesgau. They have given him a shoot of his own
of about 2,000 acres and he has stag, wild boar, pheasant, hare,
rabbits, roe deer and pigeons and duck. They are shooting pigeons
now, ducks come later and pheasants in November. They can hunt
wild boar already and he has shooting rights in other shoots that
total more than 20,000 acres.

I had hoped to go over and shoot with him this fall to take a
vacation but Mary's father had a return of that old trouble he had
in Chicago and Mary had to go over to Gulfport. She only had to
stay about a week and he is out of the hospital now. But we never
know when he may have to go back in and she have to go over
again. So I will have to stand by here. At least through Sept. and
October.

I've re written 76,000 words (cut, revised etc. and written new
of the first part of my book that I stopped on when you were laid
up that summer. The second part is about 35,000 and the third is
44,000 and the last one, that I wrote right after you and Henny left
here last New Years is 22,000. The third and the last parts won't
have to have any re writing at all practically. But will have to do
quite a lot of the second part. But I'm tired now and stale and I want
to take some sort of a rest or vacation and hit the going over fresh.

The pool has been wonderful and clean and cool all summer.
Who has had a rough time with the heat is poor Black Dog. But
pretty soon we'll get northers again.

I hope your painting is going good old Mouse and that you and Henny didn't have too uncomfortable a summer. Have you ever gotten to the Prado yet? Madrid should be nice after the middle of September. I am so glad you got the extension and I hope you will get another one.

When and if you get this letter let's try and keep good contact because I might still be able to get over while you and Henny are in Europe.

Best love to Henny. Mary sends her love and so does Gianfranco.

Much love
Papa.

THE PAINTING GOES MUCH SMOOTHER

To EH, September 18, 1951
Los Boliches, Spain

Dear Papa,

Please forgive me for being so poor on letter writing for the last two months. Have been in Malaga all the time but the last week, when we moved down the coast about thirty miles towards Algeciras to a town a little bit smaller than San Francisco de Paula. The house has a big window on the water and the second day we came there was a school of porpoises playing about two hundred yards from the beach, but have not seen them again since then. In the morning every day, you can look out and see someone walking back pulling up his pants after doing his morning business on the beach. "Maria, donde sale la porquaria del pueblo?" long, thoughtful pause. "Casi por todas partes."[2]

Have not heard much from people but mother sent me a picture of Gig and Jane, and they both looked very good. Mother spent the summer out in Los Angeles with Aunt Jinny and I think they all had a fine time.

---

2   Spanish for "'Maria, where does the crap of the town go?' long, thoughtful pause. 'Almost everywhere.'"

Now that I am more in the country, the painting is going much better. Go out in the morning and the evening, for the middle of the day is still too bright. Have found it pays to work carefully on the preliminary drawing; afterwards the painting goes much smoother.

Best to Finca, love to Mary and Gianfranco. Henny sends love.

Much love,
Mouse

THE FAT BOOK VS. THE PUFFY

To EH, September 28, 1951
Los Boliches, Spain

Dear Papa,

Thank you for very cheering letter of the 16th. Would be wonderful
If you did come over and we could all get together on those 20,000
Frieburg acres, for the little bit I've seen of Germany impressed me as
the best hunting country in Western Europe the lack of democracy and
respect for the law, even conservation laws, has kept game as thick
as it was in the 1830's, when firearms suddenly began to exterminate
the bigger game, once the common people, who did not have the sense
of property reservation of the old estate holders could get guns. It's
true isn't it that the until recently undemocratic countries of Europe,
England (in the shooting sense), Germany, Poland, Hungary etc. the
shooting was the best? Added to this, no Germans have been allowed
to have firearms for six years, and I remember when we were fishing
with Bum, a big red fox came out of the woods cross the river and
walked self confidently across the fields, usually a wary beast.

Much thanks also for $500., on which two can live for more
than six months in Spain, much to the disgrace, I must add of the
human race, for the wages are even lower than the prices. What
ever currency It comes through in, I think it can be negotiated in
Tangiers, where there are English Jews skilled in the trade.

The draft permission I have now expires on the first of December, but I don't know what the prospects of getting another are. My own opinion is that there wont be any war with Russians ever, but infinite ones with unknown tongues and tribes. I wonder why the unknown tribes don't demand that the Ruskies take at least as active a part in the struggle as we do. If they don't, I think there is hope in U.T. enthusiasm slacking off.

Very happy about progress of book. Spanish is good enough to read Cervantes now and I think the big fat book which goes along at its own dignified, rich, and full of surprises, pace is better for the reader than any other. I hope book is a fat book of this type. My critic blood would love to go on and establish the distinction between the fat book and the puffy book (T., the glories of riding the subway, Wolfe), pero ja no tiene interes.[3]

Have been in bed all day with the grip (the grip which is being distilled in Spain it this moment, and will be shipped to the rest of the world when it has reached the proper proof) which has stopped painting for two days, but hope to begin to tomorrow. What puzzles me is the mystery of the process. One picture can be so good and next not so good.

Water is perfect for swimming, and until I got the grip was swimming two kilometers a day. Mediterranean is, under the surface, a very dull ocean compared to the Caribbean and the net fishermen here keep it swept clean close to shore. They have the old Salmonete[4] as a delicacy here. I was very pleased to see his old whiskers again.

---

3   Spanish for "but he has no interest."
4   Spanish for "red mullet."

Henny has also had her round of the grip but is all well now and even took a shower today.

Thanks for Bum's address, I had hoped he might come to Spain for the salmon fishing, but I guess he had little reason to leave what he has got now. Shotguns (made from basque steel) are very cheap here. I could send you a catalogue if you are interested; although when all said and done, German and English guns are the best. Wonder if Bum has picked up any Merkels?

Love to Mary and Gianfranco (his place sounds fine, Is it that Finca that we always use to notice with the good trees on the way to Rancho Boyeros?). Henny sends love.

Much love,
Mouse

POLITICS HERE ALL BALLED UP

To PH, September 30, 1951
Finca Vigía, Cuba

Dear Mouse:

Thanks for the good letter from Fuengirola. Sorry you had such miserable weather in Madrid. You might try it again. I agree with you about the Mantegna. I always saved it for the last. You must have seen the Heronymus Bosch and the Breughels and Teniers too. Those black Goyas that he painted when he did the Caprichios and the other wild ones used to be down in the basement where there never was any light to see them properly. I suppose the amount of reproductions that have been made do affect the effect of the pictures on you. When I first saw all those pictures, the only ones that had been reproduced much were the less interesting Velasquez and Goya and the famous local (and worthless) boys. There is a vast amount of Dutch painting by people I had never heard of that I thought was very good.

When you go out to Toledo you will see quite easily which of the Grecos in the Casa del Greco are faked. I don't think there are any fakes in the Prado of Greco.

Gig doesn't write me or answer letters. He called on the phone and said he was sending some pictures. But they never came nor did an invitation to the wedding.

Am very proud of you for writing us such good letters and I hope you are having good luck with your work, Old Mouse. I have really worked harder than I ever did even when I was writing For Whom the Bell Tolls with the worst kind of pressure put on. But let's not belly ache on Sunday morning. Leave that to the local cure.

Politics down here all balled up and don't know which way it will straighten out and if. Hevia is an honest man but I don't know whether they can elect him or not. Batista is making a giant come back and had 70,000 people out in a meeting in the Parque Central for his nomination for the Presidential Elections next summer. Last week there was talk of Prio resigning and turning the Govt. over to the Armed Forces who would turn it over to who? Or keep it. Prio denied this rumor the same night. Gran is under indictment for his regime having stolen 178,000,000.

Don't know whether you will get this, Mouse, as Lista de Correos is not such always a sound address. I'll write mother to see if you have any new address.

Best luck and see the Prado for me.

Best love to Henny from us both.

Papa

MOTHER DIED SUDDENLY

To PH, October 1, 1951
Finca Vigía, Cuba

To:
FINCA VIGÍA, SAN FRANCISCO DE PAULA, CUBA
NLT (Night Letter)
Patrick Hemingway
Lista de Correos
FUENGIROLA
Provincia Malaga
Espana

Feel terribly to share bad news but Aunt Jinny wired mother died suddenly of heart attack on coast stop will send flowers for you and Henny when burial place decided stop theres nothing for you to do except not worry about anything Mouse and keep on working well stop write me where to deposit your monthly check and will look after all finances stop deepest sympathy and all our love Papa

Sender E. Hemingway Finca
Vigía San Francisco de Paula.

MOTHER WAS PERFECT TO ME

To EH, October 6, 1951
Los Boliches, Spain

Dear Papa,

Thank you for sending wire so quickly. Have heard nothing more except two telegrams of sympathy, one from Jay Allen's son Michael and the other from Shanley, but I know it takes five days for letters to get here at the least. Both Henny and I very much appreciate your sending the flowers, for I don't think we will know in time where Mother is or where she will be buried. I would also be grateful if you would have Don Andres say a mass for her. I have had it done here, but I don't know the priest and he doesn't know Mother.

A person can't be perfect in their relations with everybody, it's too complicated, but I do know Mother was perfect to me and that I could never have been able to do enough for her and the way it has turned out I have not done anything at all for her. Papa, she was wonderful the way she could do anything. I remember how she used to fish with you on the Clark's Fork and how she shot the lion and what a good cook she could make, like Marium and Ada. I loved the way she dressed, without making it a life's work but the absolute pitch of the professional, and with her smart head, respect for education, wit, and a nice sharp fierceness when she used it, like a bee sting, she was more like a Frenchwoman than an

American. I know she was a good newspaperwoman for both Elmer Davis and Charlie Ross both came to talk with her whenever they were in Key West and just a couple of years ago she had a man from the Daily News eating out of her hand and when he went back to New York to write a piece called "Key West, the Singapor of America", every other word was "as Pauline said". She was also very tolerant of second rate people and never valued herself as intrinsically better than anyone else although she would not always enjoy them. Please excuse me for writing all this, but you are probably the only person besides myself who know it is all true and appreciate it objectively.

Please thank Mary for her sympathy, I know mother liked her very much, and thanks to everyone else. Thank you very much about the money. Will write about this in my next letter.

Much love,
Patrick / Mouse

SINK OR SWIM ON MY OWN

To EH, November 13, 1951
Key West, Florida

Dear Papa,

I got your letter today as it was held up by being included with
Mother's mail, which goes to Mr. Harris, but this doesn't excuse my
not writing sooner. It has been a very busy and hectic week with
Gig and Jane getting off and Aunt Jinny deciding what she wants
to do. I know how you feel about her and it is none of my business
to question your judgement, but I do owe her a debt of gratitude for
handling all the things connected with mother's death things I wish
I could have been able to take care of my self, but which my being
so far away made impossible. She is going up to New York to see a
doctor and also be present at a friends wedding (Mrs. Culbertson),
and I had at first hoped we might go to see Mathew Herold about
Mothers trust fund and Warner Hudnut Stock, about which he
seems to be the person best informed. From what you said over the
phone, I will be more reserved and ask him to write any information
he is willing to give me to Mr. Harris so that there will be some
written record, but would like to put off making the decision of Mr.
Rice and the watching brief until I had at least seen Mr. Herold
myself. Henny and I plan to leave with Aunt Jinny tomorrow by
car to Miami (Mrs. Thompson is going to drive us up) spend the
night there and arrive by plane in New York Thursday afternoon.

We will spend about three days in New York, two in Baltimore with Henny's parents, and then come back to Key West, spend a couple of days doing unpacking and getting painting stuff in shape (which we still haven't had time to do) and would love to come over to Finca sometime during the last week in November or whenever we may.

Thanks very much for the dope on the draft and enlistment. I talked with a recruiting sergeant here in Key West and found out that the period of enlistment for the Army is three years as compared with four in the Navy and Air Corps, but that there are no concrete advantages in enlistment over being drafted except in the attitude of the people that are handling you. This didn't seem enough to me, so have decided to sit tight at least until the end of the month, for up until the 30th of November, I can still enlist even after I have had my preinduction physical, up until I receive my actual notice of induction.

If any thing comes up that you need to get in touch with us before we get back, we will be staying with or seeing Michael Allen, 21 Washington Square North all the time we are in New York.

Papa, I hope I am not being an officious twerp in this business. I feel that at the age of twenty three (not an advanced age in any way, of course) I must sink or swim in regard to my own business. When I am acting stupid or disrespectful, please tell me and tell me plainly. I am not as talented or interesting as Mr. Giggy, but I want to be a dutiful son to you, good brother to Gig (not so easy!), a husband to Henny, as good a friend of Mary as she was of Mother, a favorite nephew to Aunt Jinny, a very proud younger brother of Bum, and what time's left over, a painter.

> Will write from New York,
> Much Love,
> Mouse

NO MORE OF A DISGRACE

To PH, November 24, 1951
Finca Vigía, Cuba

Dear Mouse:

Am sending over with Henny the legalized medical certificate of Dr. Vega who was the senior physician in charge of your illness that followed the concussion you had in Key West. Both Dr. Jose Luis Herrera and Dr. Vega feel that you should present this certificate at your pre induction physical examination.

Please explain to the Dr. who examines you that you have no desire to evade military service and the two Doctor's have no wish for you to evade military service. But it is dishonest to the army not to tell them you had this illness which Jose Luis Herrara, who has had much military experience, believes disqualifies you for service.

Dr. Stettmeir is in Santiago de Cuba or I would have consulted with him as well. If the examining physician wishes me to send him any further data about your concussion and subsequent illness I will be glad to do so. The translation made by Roberto is to serve as an aid in case the examining physician does not read Spanish. They can have an official translation made in English.

I know from personal observation at the front and from the books I have read since the great amount of men who became casualties through not being properly screened in their physical examinations. It is no disgrace to inform an examining physician of an illness that you have had. I think you are one of the bravest and finest people I have ever known and at the same time I do not believe that you are fit for military service at this time. It is no more of a disgrace than for a fine horse to have had an accident and not be fit to race. You are fit for many other things and I know that you will do them well.

Excuse this letter sounding formal. It was fine seeing Henny and I hope we will see you soon too.

I hope I have handled this certificate thing properly. After all there is only one way to do things: the honest and straight way. Don't be too impressed by your imposing sounding symptoms. You conquered all of them as the certificate proves. And don't worry about any of this nor about the finances nor estate settlement nor anything. I've looked at your paintings several times and think they are sound and really first rate.

Much love from Mary and
Papa.

MENTAL HEALTH EXCELLENT

To EH, November 27, 1951
Key West, Florida

Dearest Papa,

I hope my sudden phone call did not interfere too much with
your work, and you know how much I appreciate your sense of
responsibility and concern over what happens to all three of
your children. This concussion, parafrenia, amnesia, and what
all business is just one more thing that has to be handled much
faster than it should be, like all problems. When I came out of
the examination on Monday, I was thinking like a good potential
soldier that I should do what I was told: get a letter from the
doctor who treated me for my concussion concerning my inability
to remember the circumstances of my illness, or to put it more
formally, my amnesia. It never occurred to me think further and
realize that they would probably not have asked me for such a
letter had I shown them my certificate which contains much more
evidence of former mental derangement than simple amnesia and
undoubtably disqualifies me from ever firing even a cap gun in
anger. I can imagine the concern of the combat rifleman knowing
that he is backed up by a parafrenic buddy ready to revert to his
former light hearted but difficult self on the administration of

the proper traumatic shock and the likewise heartfelt concern of Government Insurance at the prospect of paying my way through Mental Hospital, more expensive than college because it can last more than four years, although, of course, there is no text book allowance. That I did not present my certificate, it was probably due to pure confusion and timidness (not necessarily signs of mental disorder) and I will now send it to them together with a statement of my mental record since I was pronounced cured. For my own personal protection I should point out that I graduated with great praise only five months ago from a leading American University, where I met all requirements, both mental and physical and that I feel my present state of mental health to be excellent. The only thing that I don't think I do as well as before I was sick are problems in addition subtraction and long division, but I think this is due to a new conviction that it is easier to leave these problems to the machines so well qualified to handle them. Dear Papa, I am very sorry you have had to bother with all this, soon it may be all cleared up and we can have a little fun. Mr. Sully seems to want to come over to see you. He says: "Goddamn, I'd like to go over to see Ernest and talk to him about the place, Goddamn."

If you worry about my getting excited, you should remember that it might be nothing more significant than my temprement. No one thought there was anything serious in the way Mr. LaGuardia used to get excited. If your confidence in me is shaken, remember that I have been completely in control of my own life for the past three years and that I have made those years healthy and happy for my self (on other people's money, of course, and a lot of it yours, over $2000. since I've been of age) using nobody's judgement but my own and other's advice. I no longer have other's advice, but I have yours, which I respect but don't feel I have a constant and uninterrupted right to it.

Much love to Mary and hope Sinsky is well

Much love

(.) (.) (.) (.)

SHOOTING NEAR A NUDIST COLONY

To EH, January 28, 1952
Key West, Florida

Dear Papa,

Mr. Thompson took me up with him to hunt quail behind
Homestead last Sunday. The country is very tough. Cut over pine
with the water pocked flint ground that eats up shoes. They had
good dogs, for we didn't lose a cripple.[5] The best shooting we had
was close by a nudist colony, where we put up a big covey that
hadn't been shot at all year. I was with another man, and we each
got one bird as we flushed the covey and then picked up seven
more as we worked the singles. The singles really stuck close.
We had to kick them out with our feet and a couple went right
between our legs.

I will try and get the solunar tables today.

Love to Mary

Much love
Mouse

---

5   Wounded birds

GOOD LUCK DID NOT BAG A NUDIST

To PH, February 5, 1952
Fina Vigia, Cuba

Dear Mouse:

Glad you got some quail shooting. Good luck you didn't bag a
nudist with your second barrel. They shot the International pigeon
shoots here. El Chino won two of them and Jose Naria Cuervo
the other. I didn't shoot as couldn't afford to shoot the necessary
amount of pigeons it would have taken to get into form after a
years lay off. They were charging a dollar a bird for any practice
shoots and wouldn't let you bring your own birds. Quintero has
the pigeon supply racket tied up tight. Poli could have gotten any
amount of birds at half that price.

Sinsky much much better and Don Andres better in health
and in morale. We had a strange type of baby cyclone last saturday
that probably moved up through you too. It blew about 55 miles
from the south with heavy rain and then after blowing about three
hours suddenly stopped to a dead calm. Didn't do any damage and
the rain was good for the Finca.

There has been a steady and over running stream of people
from the north who have letters of introduction or are old friends
and I am going down the coast for a week in the boat to Paraiso as
soon as there is good weather. Have to get some sort of a vacation
before I start re writing.

No answer from Gig since I wrote him after talking to you that morning.

I'd hoped to get a real vacation but I guess I will just have to settle for a week down the coast. Still any day in the boat on the water makes me feel better. Have had one day on the sea since September.

If anything comes up and I do not answer promptly it will be because I hope to be away at least a week starting tomorrow or Friday February 7th.

Mary sends her love to you both. So do I. Paraiso Kiss

Papa.

SENDING OFF BOOKS AND MANUSCRIPTS

To EH, February 26, 1952
Key West, Florida

Dear Papa,

I am sending off the books and manuscripts to you today. There was no manuscript of poems that I could find. It might turn up later, but I doubt it, for I have gone over everything thoroughly. In the bookshelves I also ran across a book by Ezra Pound with a dedication to you in ink by the author and have put it in the package too. I hope you were not put out any by my slowness in getting these off to you.

Very sorry to hear about Mr. Scribner's death. Who will take his place in the Company? Dawn Powell is here, and she says she is giving up Scribners as her publisher.

About the money you pay to Gig, I don't think it is any of my business, do you? I am sorry he doesn't write. From what I heard from Aunt Jinny and from Jane, both Gig and Jane went back to college as pre med students in February. Ada is helping them out with the baby.[6] I am enclosing one of the photographs Jane sent us.

---

6   Lorian Hemingway, Gregory's eldest child.

Have you heard anything more from Bum and Puck? I think they intended to go first to see Hadley and Paul in New Hampshire, then head South.

Mr. Harris thinks my mother's estate should be more or less settled by the end of August.

It is terrible you had to pay duty on our present, much of which you probably didn't want anyway, especially the salmon eggs which they slipped in instead of the caviar we ordered. Please let us know what the customs was and will pay back.

My love to you and Mary,
Mouse
(.) (.) (.) (.)

NOT IN THE STORAGE BUSINESS

To EH, February 29, 1952
Key West, Florida

Dear Papa,

It was stupy of me to risk sending the books and manuscripts, but I did send them by registered air mail (#10401, sent from Key West post office, February 25) and wrapped them very carefully and sealed them with scotch tape. Here is the list to check with the contents of the package. There is only one package:

Three Stories. Ten Poems, Contact Publishing Co., 1922 In Our Time, Three Mountains Press, 1924

"In Another Country", a story by Ernest Hemingway, typewritten manuscript or perhaps a carbon copy.

"In Another Country", part two, typewritten manuscript or perhaps a carbon copy.

"Benchley: The Image and The Man", typewritten manuscript.

Death in the Afternoon, parts of a typewritten manuscript, first chapter etc.

These were all together in the parchment trunk. I also ran across book by Ezra Pound in the bookshelves which is certainly yours and thought you might like to have it. There are still quite a few books scattered through the bookshelves that have your signature in them and which you might have forgotten to tell

Bruce to get when he originally sent all the books over, or he might have overlooked them. I can gather these together and have them crated for shipment to you or can hand them over to whoever you wish for safekeeping. These books, the Spanish chair and table, and the Quintanilla portrait are everything of yours in the house that I can think of, but if there is anything else that you can think of that I've forgotten, please let me know so that I can look out for them and do with them what you wish me to do. If you want someone else to take care of them, please don't hesitate to do so, for fear of hurting my feelings. They might very well be safer, for I am not in the storage business, only an untalented amateur. Joke.

Papa, I know there are a lot of worthless people in the world, and they should be treated accordingly. If you think I am a worthless person, that I am sitting over here loafing, with designs on your property, tell me so, and I will know clearly what I am and make some effort to do better. I on the other hand, think I am here because my mother's estate is being handled in this town, it is cheaper for me to stay in one spot than to travel when my mind is not made up as to my future. It is necessary for me to give a certain impression of stability when my brother is a minor and to a certain degree the ignorant of his responsibilities, and I require a certain cooling off atmosphere where I am Independent and yet the surroundings are familiar. This place here has been my home, as much as the Finca for the last twenty years. I am nervous and hesitant about leaving it for good. I don't want to make quick or bad decisions. It is quite true that I am too cautious, too self conscious of the impression I make on other people, just as Gig is too reckless and to ignorant or careless of the impression he makes on other people. Please excuse all this self justification. I think we have always been good friends, and I think we both have one thing very much in common, that we go on doing something that really does not appeal to us at all because we don't want to do any thing wrong, and then we really blow up.

> Much love,
> Mouse
> (.) (.) (.)

YOUR FRIEND FROM HARVARD

To PH, April 1, 1952
Finca Vigía, Cuba

Dear Mouse:

Your friend from Harvard came here un announced and un explained by you, and I spent all the time at his and my disposal discussing (seriously god help me) his writing. If you have read it you must have an opinion of it. I would like to hear it. He seemed to have the good qualities of the Saxon. They are, however negative, preferable to the Bavarian.

Mary has asked some Bemedji friend of hers to call on you with his wife. Please don't think I have sent them. But I am sure you will be polite to them. If they are friends of Mary I am sure they are nice. But I don't want to bother you or Henny.

Sent Gregory his April check. He wrote me nothing after his two insulting letters and his receipt of previous check.

MAKE YOUR JUDGMENTS

To PH, April 13, 1952

Finca Vigía, Cuba

Dear Mouse:

Thanks for Leicester's address and the two checks, which came yesterday. I sent Gig's check to him immediately. He had not acknowledged any checks nor written anything since his insulting letter. But my check to him was in the cancelled checks I received so he received it and cashed it o.k. That was his check for March First. I suppose the cancelled check for April will be along in May. It is pleasant to know that this one sided correspondence will terminate in November.

If you had planned to leave Key West before the end of April you certainly have no obligation to wait on for Bumby when he does not communicate. I hear nothing from him either and do not know if he has left Europe. Meantime I stay here waiting for him when I could have finished my vacation.

Why don't you send a cable to his last military address asking when to expect him? For all I know, now, he may not even be coming.

Neither he nor Gregory ever communicate unless they need money or want something. But in this case Bumby's orders may have been changed and it is a job moving a wife and small child from Europe with household goods and maybe he has just been careless. Carelessness is damned annoying. But Bum has always had a good heart and been a good friend and I am proud of him in many ways and forgive him for being a sloppy correspondent. And when he does something wrong Bumby knows it and is sorry. But I wish he would write you and write me.

A month out of anybody's life hanging around adapting all your plans to someone else who does not even bother to write is damned annoying. I'm awfully sorry you have had to put up with it. Uncertainty is the worst thing.

Don't worry about the Solunar's. There was a 25 (cent sign) standard pamphlet with a conversion table. But if it is not for sale in Key West we can get it through N.Y. We are still eating the marvellous kippered herring you and Henny sent. They are the best I've ever eaten and I eat them skin bones and all. One the last trip we caught several hundred pounds of beautiful yellowtail, red and nassau groupers and big pargo trolling over the coral heads with the Tin Kid using a tiny feather and pork rind. Gregorio and I caught 19 big yellow tail and mutton fish in an hour and a half one day. The biggest mutton fish was 14 lbs. On very light tackle they were wonderful fun.

It's blowing a heavy south breeze today (Easter Sunday) but I hope to get out tomorrow. The deal I hope to make some money from is still held up. But everyone says it is sure and the people who have read it like the stuff very much. It will be a really good one if it comes through. In the meantime I wish we would get this uncertainty about Mr. Bumby over so that I can either finish vacation or settle into work.

Mary sends her love to you and Henny. That character who was over here said that the infection in Henny's leg had never healed. I hope that is not true and that it is being treated properly. Dr. Kohly said it should never have lasted this long and should have been healed months ago. Please let me know about this so that we won't worry.

Best love to you both,
Papa

BUM STOPPED BY

To EH, June 7, 1952
Piggott, Arkansas

Dear Papa,

I got a nice letter from Mr. Breit and answered it immediately. I hope he can use some of the dope.

I've been learning how to run a tractor the last week and can do it pretty well now, although I have trouble figuring out how to skip rows. Cultivating is of course the lightest plowing, but with the new tractors with hydraulic lifts, even handling three bottom breaking plows isn't too hard work. There are hardly any mules or horses up here and what there are they use only for planting with the drill. Two evenings ago, over in a field of soybeans I was helping to plow, there were two foxes. They looked like two big squirrels when they moved, and their white fronts flashed everytime they sat up turned our way. They come out to catch the rabbits when these get out in the open to eat the young bean sprouts. Lots of doves and I notice quite a few fields of young rice, so there ought to be some dove shooting in the all.

Bum stopped by for a day and wants to go to Africa and buy a farm and me come with him. Are there any hill farms that you can have a balanced program instead of one cash crop like cotton, sysal or coffee? Please write, for it is not very exciting here.

Much Love,
Mouse

AFRICA CAN ALWAYS DEFEAT YOU

To PH, June 11, 1952
Finca Vigía, Cuba

Dear Moose:

Thanks very much for the letter and for writing Mr. Breit and
for all the gen. I was pretty sure we were right about selling the
first place but then there were all the imponderables and my wish
for you to do what you thought best. It is a terribly rough system
under which one may command. But I never wanted to command
anyway. But you know how the old Spanish system of the junta
and the consejo de guerra before any decision is taken is pretty
fatal. And when three people have to agree on what shall be done
and one of them won't show nor answer nor take any responsibility
it gets fantastic for one who is trying to use the head and do what
the others want. Don't worry too much about the tax angle. Tax
angles are like mosquitoes on Cayo Romano. You guys became
30% owners of the property when Mother died. But I had been a
complete owner until divorce and then a 40 percent owner and I
can remember when I made a dollar a word in Spain (but was shot
at plenty for same) and all the money went into mother's bank
account never touched by me. When I came back from Spain I
thought we had a lot of money. But it had all gone into house and
swimming pool. Later Mother spent much more on the house. But
I was always paying. But the huge spending was from the start

on when it was an abandoned, unfenced lot with an abandoned house and trucks parked in the back. The furniture and the nice things that made it a good home I earned with all the different books. The popular theory that I was a bum who was picked up from poverty and supported on Pfeiffer money always seemed to me sort of strange when I married Mother after I had written The Sun Also Rises which I followed with Men Without Women, Death In The Afternoon, Winner Take Nothing, To Have and Have Not, and For Whom The Bell Tolls and also gave her 500 shares of stock in Esquire Magazine and every time Uncle Gus gave us a present I gave him a Manuscript which was at least double the value of the present. This was the value of the manuscripts at the time they were given. Now they are much more valuable. Uncle Gus wrote me, and I have the letters, that he was only holding them for his enjoyment until his death and then they would be returned to me. But I suppose now they are in the hands of The Committee if they have not been sold or given away to a University, after appraisal, to obtain a tax benefit.

Mrs. Stevens and the other vermin certainly had a wonderful thing to eat on. It is true that I was an unfaithful husband and was divorced as such with punitive alimony. But I was faithful for seven years under a regime which would not permit any form of birth control (none; period) and with six years of imposed coitus interruptus. You are married and know what that means. I loved Mother and admired her and loved her truly more than I ever loved anyone in all my life. But I think I was beaten by a system and my own inability to stick it out. However I did last six years at that and without complaint. Nor with any now except that I think the system was barbarous.

The hell with all that. Glad you saw Bum. He hasn't seen fit to write us although we have heard of him now through you and through Sun Valley.

About Africa: I do not know how much it has changed. It is a continent that can always defeat you in farming with the failure of the monsoon, the arrival of the locusts etc. But it is a lovely country to live in and to paint and there are nice people that Henny would like and that would like Henny. I think you could live there on a break even basis and have the shooting and the fishing that we love. I would rather live there than any other place in the world.

At present we are living under a military dictatorship and you know that I have never been very good at that metier. If you guys went to Africa I would join you.

Hope this letter will be cheery. Roberto now is supposed to live. He lost about three litres and a half of blood. (All replaced.) When he was dying he had great dignity and cheerfulness and sent a fine message to you. I never saw a man die better and recover. If any hitch in recovery will send the message.

Don't worry about 907 Whitehead. I am eating ok. We have money for plasma and 907 has now evidently become an investment. An investment, in these days, ranks somewhere between an ulcer and carcinoma. I wish I would have had my letters and my manuscripts. But I hope to put the people in jail who stole them. They are all traceable. It will be a troublesome job but maybe in my old days will be trouble. Gregory's wife wrote last month to give the new address for the monthly check. She wrote a very nice and friendly letter and explained about how Gregory was too busy to write. It seems he has some problem with Chemistry. I am always happy that he never mastered Physics so that he cannot sell the Secret of the Atom to any of his friends.

In the tournament Elicin and I will fish together and Mary is fishing in the Tin Kid with Gianfranco. They have it really tough and I wish they had the Pilar. But it is a thing of pride with Mary and she has two good fish under her belt for training. She caught lots of fish before and has been swimming an 880 every day. Also neither she nor Gianfranco mind the sun. But 12 hours a day for three days is rough. I will try to yank them if it gets too tough. There is a terrific heavy blue current, easy brisa, and fish of every size and kind.

Mooser I wish you were here and we were fishing together. I would rather fish with you and shoot with you than anybody that I have ever known since I was a boy and this is not because we are related.

Best love always to Henny and to you from Mary and I and from Sinsky who was here yesterday and from Gianfranco. Thank you again for being to prompt and good in answering Mr. Breit.

Papa

THE HEAT GOT TOO BAD

To EH, July 6, 1952
Los Angeles, California

Dear Papa,

The heat got too bad in Arkansas for Henny, So we left the 15th
of June for here by way of Laramie and Twin Falls. In Laramie I
talked to Marjorie Cooper, whom we took out to lunch and asked
about Africa. Her son looks just like Colonel Cooper and both the
children speak Swahili. There is a farm for sale, for 15,000 pounds,
very near to Colonel Cooper's farm, and it already has a house and
the coffee trees planted. I think it would be worth looking at. When
I saw Puck in Twin Falls she said that Bum was very pleased
with his new job at Fort Brag, which is operations instead of aide
work, and so he may not want to get out of the Army in December.
I would love it if he also came to Africa with me, but it is more of a
risky business with him than with me and Henny. Muffet looks a
lot like Bum's mother, but her grandparents had been feeding her
too much. I have not seen my other niece, for both Jane and Lorian
have been visiting Jane's mother in Memphis, and we just missed
them when we arrived out here. Gig is in very good shape. He got
me a job with a British mechanic so that I could learn something
about gasoline motors, for according to Mrs. Cooper, the service on
tractors and cars is not too good in Tanganyika.

Henny was feeling pretty rocky towards the end in Arkansas and the trip across the country. We made Denver in two driving days from Piggott, but she had to spend a day in bed in Kansas City. She is ok now, but it has been a hundred and seven in Arkansas the last week! The dry June they were so pleased with is turning into a drought and they need rain.

My plans are uncertain at the moment for I am waiting to hear from Bum as to whether he is going to get out of the Army or not. Until I hear, I will stay here and work with the mechanic. Boats leave pretty regularly for Mombassa, the next is August 30, Takes five weeks and costs $650.00.

Much love,
Mouse

JUDGE THE COUNTRY BEFORE THE RAINS

To PH and Gregory, July 10, 1952
Finca Vigía

Dear Mouse and Gig:

Thanks very much for your letters and you, Gig, for Bum's address. Excuse me writing a combined letter but there is a lot of gen I should give you both as soon as possible. So will get this off.

Bum was down here last Friday, Sat. and left again for Bragg Sunday morning. He has decided to stay in the army and go for regular army. I think it is a wise decision since he can have no career in civil life as long as he is a reserve officer. He will always be subject to call, and since he is young and well trained as a specialist in the army he would be subject to call for many years. He has made SUPERIOR consistently for the last two years on his French job. If he makes the permanent rank of Captain in the regular army he could make Col. or B.G. in war time. Anyway he will be advancing steadily with his card being punched in the machine that takes the SUPERIOR cards. He made the decision before he came down to see me and I agreed with it.

That's the gen on Bum. He was fine, sound, in good spirits but a little over weight. He was going to do field problems and that will take care of the weight. We went out in the boat and of course got nothing for the first time in weeks. He is coming down with Puck and his daughter later. They were to join him on the 13th of July.

If you are planning to go out August 20th and it takes Six weeks voyage you would not have much time to judge the country and look it over before the rains. But if you wanted to know what it was like on a full year basis you could go through the month and half of rain and then see the country afterwards. But it would doubtless be as unpleasant and different as when the season changes at Key West. There is no place that I know in the world where the climate does not become unpleasantly hot or unpleasantly cold at some time. But you either have to select the good times for various countries or have the fortitude to stick it when it gets bad. To know that it is bad at certain times is a great advantage so that you can avoid it. But I don't see how, Mouse, you can go out to East Africa leaving August 20th and take six weeks for the voyage and have time to get any sort of thorough look at the country and not hit the smaller rainy season.

So much for that. I did not like the country around Col. Cooper's farm at all when we were there. It was never a place I would have picked to live. But you will see all that when you get out there. I think you ought to look into various parts of Kenya as well as Tangauyika. I would say that there is country in East Africa that is much nicer than that country around Babati where Dick lived as the old days Clark's Fork country was nicer than, say, Cody. But there have been lots of changes. Game has been exterminated in many areas where it was plentiful to help the settlers etc. You can only judge the part of the country that you would want to live in but looking it over thoroughly and it would be tragic for the short rains to come and have someone think "This is the way Africa is."

I'd suggest you see Philip Perceval, who was a good friend of Mother's and of mine, and if possible stay a few days at his place and have him tell you about the different parts of the country; their advantages and disadvantages and arrange for you to stay as paying guests at somebody's farm. You could then travel and look around yourselves. But truly I think you will find places where you would rather live and farm than the Babati country. In any case don't buy a place in a hurry nor figuring that you can do more than make a living. You don't want to get into something where you will have to work so hard to protect your capital that you can never take time off to handle a rod or a gun. If you can have a life that is comfortable and healthy and pleasant and that you can break even on then anything you make as money is to the good.

Think I better send this now so you get this for what it is worth.

Will write both you and Gig. Must also write Bum and Miss Mary. Her parents are both in bad shape although her father is better temporarily. She is still feeling the situation out in the first letter I had from her today.

> Much love to all,
> Papa.

If you are going to look the African thing over, Mouse, the thing to do is get out there. But I thought I should give you the gen, as I remembered it, about the rains.

I HAVE PASSAGE ON A FREIGHTER

To EH, August 12, 1952
New York, New York

Dear Papa,

I have passage on a freighter now scheduled to leave on the 29th
of this month, and since it will take me something over a month
to get to Mombasa, I will probably hit the small rainy season right
on the nose. I am still waiting for the old on my application for
an immigrant's visa, and, of course, there is a chance this might
not come through in time for me to take the boat. I made the
application for Kenya Colony rather than Tanganykca, after what
you said about the Babati country, and because I think it would
be easier to find a small, mixed crop farm a close enough to the big
center of European settlement so that there would be a market for
produce there instead of having to depend on the European prices
for coffee and flax, which have made so many people go broke. I
think your idea of going to see Mr. Percival very good, and I will go
very easy on buying a place. From all I can learn, land prices are
inflated in Kenya now, because of the large number of people who
have gone out there since the War. This is a shame, for from what I
have read about the unsteady rainfall and the locusts, it is not the
Ideal farming country, to say nothing of the very long distances to
any world markets.

We had a very nice visit with Gig, but we didn't see Jane, who was away visiting her mother in Memphis. Gig seemed in good shape, still intent on being a doctor, and not at all self centered like he has been for the last few years. He is not all mixed up with the crazy element on the coast, but has a nice house, only a few blocks from the University. The family next door have two peacocks, and it was wonderful to hear that old noise at night again. Gig has also joined the ROTC, in an infantry outfit, so that he will have his commission when he graduates from college. I think he is having a pretty lonely fight with his trouble, especially at night, but he keeps it completely to himself, and I didn't talk to him about it at all, especially since he goes to the doctor every week, and I know nothing about it.

We will be here in New York until my boat sails, and Henny will keep the apartment until the Fall, when she goes down to Key West to pick out the things to go to Africa, and then she will come out to meet me. I hope to have some sort of arrangement by then.

Tell Mary we are across from the American Orchid Society, if she wants any dope.

Much Love,
Mouse

Excuse stupid letter. Will do better next time.

A LITTLE NERVOUS ABOUT AFRICA

To EH, August 27, 1952
New York, New York

Dear Papa,

All the red tape is over, although I have to go and have my vaccination card stamped by the Public Health Service tomorrow, and I will sail day after tomorrow. Here is all the address gen, which you might not have been able to hear on the phone, for there were times when your voice came over very weak and I suppose mine did too.

From what I have been able to read up on, I think I would like to find a place in the high country north west of Nairobi, suitable for maize with a small acreage in coffee. On that sort of a place you can have cows and pigs, vegetables, and a small cash income from coffee to pay the necessary cash expenditures for taxes, wages etc. However, my main consideration is finding a pleasant country to live, with some game left in it. I certainly do not want to get mixed up in some large plantation crop, for in the long run this means ruin to anyone who cannot operate on a very big scale. But all this must be based on actually seeing the country, and so don't pay much attention to what I say now, before seeing it. I am very glad that I at least had some experience in Arkansas, which, although it is not the beauty spot of America, is a stronghold of practical and non gentleman farming.

Both Henny and I are in good shape, but of course a little nervous about Africa. You must be very busy with book coming out, but I know it will be success, for everybody is talking about it here. Eizenhower made a dismal impression with his speech to the American Legion here. Even his staunchest supporters thought that it lacked the element of greatness they had been hoping for.

Love to Mary.

Much love,
Mouse

WORTH 1,000 NEWSPAPER REPORTS

To PH, September 22, 1952
Finca Vigía, Cuba

Dear Moose:

Hope you had a good trip. You must have needed plenty of reading matter. I cabled and wrote Philip Perceval and told him the boat you were getting in on and also that you would get in touch with him.

Mary had a letter from Henny today saying that she had been trying to telephone you at Joeburg to come home because the mao mao business only "broke" (her words) after you left and that while she was sure Pat could take care of himself there was certainly no question now of going to some remote part of the country.

As you know, Mouse, a reconnaisance sur le terrain is worth a thousand newspaper reports For instance you can read in the papers how orderly and calm everything is in some place and no mention of a second armed robbery in two months. Bad one. Nor of Dick Hill having to shoot it out for an hour with a band who stole all his turkeys and were back for a thousand chickens. Nor the robberies that go on every night.

Henny is worked up about something she read in the papers. We talked about it on the phone. You and I. If things are bad out there you will know all about it after you've been there. In the meantime look around, have some fun, and get some good shooting.

It would be a crime to go to Africa and not have some good
shooting even if the only game left was the elusive moa moa (if mis
spell them often enough will get it right). If you like it, and all it is
is dangerous, let me know and I'll come out with you. When things
are bad I don't have to take seconal to sleep well. But you have a
good look at it and enjoy it. And don't let any woman no matter
how much you love her nor how fine she is ever yank you out of a
duck blind when ducks are coming in nor have you cut off a big fish
to be home in time for supper nor get you to give up painting nor
anything else.

If you hear from Henny that she lost a baby that is untrue.
She wrote me in early September that she was going to have a
baby in April. Ni Winchell predicts blessed events that far ahead.
She's just written Mary that she has lost the baby. The actual
phrase is that she missed a period. Many women miss one or two
periods. I've seen it from change in altitude, from nervousness,
from many things. But usually it means that their insides are
not properly organized. A month ago Miss Mary was sure that we
were going to have a baby and she was so happy and I felt happy
about her being happy. But I knew it was impossible because
I was present giving the plasma when she had the tubular
pregnancy in Casper that time and nearly died and saw the
condition of the other fallopian tube and knew she would never
have a baby. This was confirmed, finally, by the best specialist in
N.Y. at considerable expense and great pain. I know nothing about
Henny's physical condition. I was only, as you father, telling you
not to worry about missing periods as anything except such. They
could be a sign of other conditions. But many women miss one of
two without being pregnant. Don't know how I ever got into this
obstetrical paragraph but a husband of some 32 years standing

and was turning over to you whatever knowledge I had that might be useful so you wouldn't worry. In New York any woman with any money will find a doctor willing and anxious to explore her insides at length.

In pioneer days men sometimes had 12 wives without divorces. Working conditions for women have picked up tremendously. For men too. But there are still some of the old problems left. Let's leave it alone.

Christ I wish I were out with you now though I think it is better for you to work it out by yourself.

Book seems to be going good. About 98 percent of the reviews were favourable. Am going so good with the critics that must expect them to throw in a big counter attack soon. They're probably re grouping their armoured brains. Since dup beat them as a writer this time they'll probably open up on my personal life; that old open sewer. It is good to be a native born American citizen. Then they can't nail you, legally, on moral turpitude. Perversion I have never gone in for. But that doesn't mean they can't accuse you of it. Somebody will probably prove I was tied in with Gide all the time and that Catherine Barkley was really one of Proust's chauffers; maybe she was Bruce. Look at the evidence of that letter of mine that Bruce Brown carried around to try to obtain credit at the best hotels. It shouldn't be any effort for a research scholar to confuse Toby Bruce with Bruce Brown.

Cowardice; of course. Look how your father fled England for France to escape the buzz bombs and then fled ahead of the 3rd Army to escape from Georgie Patton. Fleeing into Germany so panic stricken that we broke through the Siegfried in our panic until the Death Wish led to Hurtgen after which, suffering from a traumatic psychosis we wandered into Luxembourg and so feeble in the brain that we opposed the intelligent designs of Dr. Van Rundstedt. Disgraceful all of it.

You can't win against the critics. But we certainly ran over them this time.

I would like to get out but I am afraid of local mao mao situation which is a bore. Two characters in the other night on a forced lock one standing by outside Miss Mary's room with my old SS dagger waiting for me to come out. Left his cigarette butts there and took the knife. The other scattering cigar ashes, prying open cabinets, pinching everything, scattering mss. Mary and I asleep after a long day on the ocean. Always come, so far, about 0330-0430 so have the traps set then and stay awake. But a man needs a good sleep to write. It is a pain in the ass.

But you look things over well and get some good shooting. Don't think any money spent on this is money lost or wasted.

Miss Mary is going up to New York day after tomorrow for a week to get away from mao maoismo (she deserves a good break) and to see some shows and have some fun and she will see Henny.

I'll try to write you a longer and funnier letter next time. If people are spooked you might pick up something good cheap. It was that way in our Indian wars but you have to remember that there were not so many Indians out west in the old days. But at one time the odds were about the same and the lines of communication longer. Work on your Swahili and if you have time on your dialects.

Have fun schatz, don't worry and please write.

Much love from Mary and me. All news from Bumby and Gig are good.

Papa

UNBELIEVABLE COUNTRY

To EH, October 15, 1952
Nairobi, Kenya

Dear Papa,

Thanks for the fine letter. They brought it out in the pilot boat and it and the entrance to the harbour was very fine indeed. Mr. Percival had gotten your wire and wrote me to the boat and so I am going out to Machakos this afternoon. But I must remember the old Italian proverb about the guest and the fish (dopo tre giorni puzza).[7]

I wish I could make some informative statements about Mau Mau, farming etc, but only got in on the twelfth after forty three days of American freighterhood. I traded in my car at Toledo, where the Willys Overland factory is, for one of their four cylinder pick up trucks with four wheel drive and brought it with me on a tryptique, so that I was able to drive up here from Mombasa in two days. They have made a national parl out of all that maneaters of Tsavo country, and at Mtito Andei I turned off to left to go to the big springs that come out of the lava and form part of headwaters of Tsavo River. It was a tropical Blue Lakes, Idaho, with crystal clear water and hippos instead of trout. Driving back further along

---

7   Italian for "after three days it stinks."

the river about five o'clock had very good luck seeing game. A lion after a heard of zebra crossed the road about eight feet from the car, and he looked all hot and excited just like Willie after the meat tied to a sting. Lots of water buck, gants gazelle, zebra, and too much dik dik. Then on the way back, when it was just starting to get dark, saw three big black elephants standing in the river. I got out of the car and was able to get within about fifty yards of them before they lifted up their trunks, spread their ears, stood rocking back and forth on their legs and then turned around and disappeared. By this time I thought Africa a very fine place. In the middle of the day had luck to see rhino lying down under a thorn tree, with just his one ear twitching and the two points of his horns in silhouette. The country of the park is mostly thick thorn scrub, but they are trying to improve it by burning so as to have the plains animals.

Yesterday I drove around the Mgono hills and the color is something like when you wear sun glasses, only without them. It is like a whole country of chinese painting, even to the iridescent birds on the tree limb. Wonderful hawks and also an eagle. It looks like the ideal falconer's country with it so open and birds like francolin and bustard. Saw three greater busterd and two ostriches on the west side of the hills.

Papa, it is an unbelievable country, as you know, and I would certainly like to live here, if it turns out to be possible.

My love to Mary and the Finca.

Much love, Mouse

I AM GOING TO LIVE HERE IF I CAN

To EH, October 17, 1952
Potha, Kenya

Dear Papa,

I have been at the Percivals' farm now for two days, and they have
been wonderful to me. He has been giving me a lot of good advice,
of which the main thing seems to be to take my time before putting
in any capital in anything. He has some land in mind in hot dry
country where he says you can hear three lions at night, rhino
and elephant which he thinks would be good for cattle provide you
were willing to gamble on finding water and he thinks you might
be interested, but he would not recommend it for me because of
the riskyness of it. As I think he wrote you, what he is interested
in is beef cattle and it is now extremely difficult to find enough
(he considers 20,000 acres a minimum) land at a reasonable
price, unless a gamble like the one mentioned above. But he is
going to introduce me to people who who are specialists in other
branches of farming, so that I can learn something about them
too. He is not very enthusiastic about plantation crops because of
the dependence on native labor and possible market fluctuations,
but he says people are really making money on them now and all
prices are too high. I am very much uncertain as to what I am
going to do, but hope to be more intelligent about this later.

DEAR PAPA

Last night a hyena got into a boma full of young calves and killed one and maimed two others and they are setting a shotgun trap for him tonight like the one their Dutchman used to get the lion a week ago, the one that was still around when he wrote you.

The first night I came, Dick Percival took me down to the river to shoot doves and it was very much like the old evening flight at the finca before they drained that country in back. We have seen quite a few francolin and sand grouse but haven't had guns along.

Papa, I think you would like it out here (of course you have seen it, and more of it than I have) if there were a good place. I certainly am going to live here if I can manage it. Swahili is giving me trouble, perhaps because I overworked my head on languages lately and have sort of resistance to more words for the same things, but I am working hard at it and it is, in theory, not a hard language. It is certainly essential for here, and it was foolish of me not to have studied it earlier.

The short rains are quite close now and last night the sunset from Mr. Percival's son in law's house was one big splash of red underneath the black of the rains to the west. With everything brown, and the coldness of the mornings and evenings and even the shade in the daytime, I keep thinking it is fall.

Papa, please write me a letter on manners, for I am not very sure of myself sometimes. I would appreciate this, and I have not learned it at the various worthless schools I have had to spend the last fifteen years of my life.

I just stood up on the veranda to stretch and four francolin flushed about a yard away.

Love to Mary.

                              Much love,
                              Mouse

BEAUTIFUL BUT A LITTLE SINISTER

To EH, November 16, 1952
Soysambu, Kenya

Dear Papa,

I think that, probably, sending the rod to Mr. Percival from Key West by air freight would be the quickest way. Let me know the price and postage and I will write you check immediately, for I want it to be my present.

I am now away from the Percivals to see as much of the country as I can before Henny and more permanent arrangements in December. I am spending a week here at the Delamere Estates with the manager, Mr. Gerald Romer, and it is a very well developed place. Yesterday I saw Lord Delamere's grave (he is buried on the place between his two wives) and the milking herds, bulls, calves, heifers etc. The day before I took a bunch of sick lambs for them to the vet lab at Kabete and also up on the Killagop, in the wheat country right at the edge of the Aberdare forest and the holing up spot of Mau Mau (didn't see any, however).

They have a secretary bird here as pet and it is very funny to see him try and bluff a little siamese kitten. The kitten was impressed by the hissing at first, but then he chased the secretary bird all over the place. There is not much game on this estate, because it is fenced off into small paddocks, but you can see the rafts of flamingoes down on lake elmenteita and the country is beautiful although a little sinister like Utah.

I think Mau Mau will still be here when you come. Country seem very peaceful, but there was an armed daylight raid on a farm near Thompson's Falls yesterday. The funniest incident so far was a farmer who, when his house was attacked, had two misfires from his pistol, ran to get his shotgun and then shot his house boy by mistake. I suppose it isn't really funny. In another place two ferocious Rhodesian ridgeback dogs bit night watchman but slept through a robbery that happened the next day.

I am pretty sure Mary will like it here.

much love,
Mouse

YOU WRITE SO CLEARLY AND WELL

To PH, November 26, 1952
Finca Vigía, Cuba

Dear Moose:

Awfully glad to get your letter from Lord Delamere's estate. You should be getting a good look at things. Every time I hear from you it makes me happy because you write so clearly and well that it is like seeing it ones self. Awfully funny incidents about the Mau Mau. On a big picture basis it is not funny at all and many individual things can be horrible and not joke able. But I never saw a war, nor any sort of a fight big or small that didn't have very comic things. Never saw anyone worth a damn who couldn't joke in a war or any sort of really bad business either.

Rice and Al Horwits are coming down here on Dec. 15 or before with a summary of moving picture offers and will try to get that sorted out. The book is selling well and by the first of the year I should be off the hook with Scribner's and all money paid back that I had to borrow for un expected tax assessments and the time when you were ill. Have all of it paid back except $21,000 and the book has earned $20,000 with the Book of the Month and the other Scribner money, already up till now, will pay the taxes on that and the taxes on the Scribner money and leave me enough to come out to Africa. Scribners expect the book to go on selling for a long time.

They have started to advertise it now and have a very fine quote from B. Berenson which made me very happy.

Bum is doing fine and working hard. He is jumping regularly now and likes it and is doing first class work in the Special Forces Group. We've asked him and his wife down for Christmas. He couldn't come before on acct. of the polio epidemic here. Maybe they have another Christmas project though and in that case will come here when we get back from Africa. Bum writes regularly and we are going to talk with him and Puck and his daughter this Sunday by some sort of short wave radio set up that he has. He really sounds wonderful.

I subscribed to the New Yorker for you care of Barclay's Bank for six months and will subscribe to any other magazines you would like. Please let me know the ones you and Henny would like.

Figure to leave whatever arms we send out with you when we go back except maybe my big double that shoot on pigeons as might have a chance to shoot in France on the way home.

Am not trying to influence your plans but if you and Henny wanted to go on a quiet and un sensational safari with Mary and me I think we could have fun.

The local Mau Maus here have suffered a set back. Four of them broke in through the barred windows of a 62 year old Gallego Bodegero and beat and tortured him (cut off the balls) to get him to tell where the 50,000 was. Then strangled him with wire. But all four were apprehended. Two are reported dead so far from the effects of the last norther. There is a chance they were our visitors. But Gregorio and the Cojimeros caught four more a few nights ago complete with booty which they had hidden in a cave high up on the hill behind the port (toward the river).

We went out in the boat yesterday to try to follow up the luck with the fish but with the new norther coming on everything was down. I foul hooked one marlin in the hump where his dorsal fin is. He started to run and jump wildly into the path of the new big fast car ferry and we had to run almost against her bows to make him sound (running up onto the line). He sounded but with the big ground swell and heavy East Wind that came up in the afternoon the hook pulled out of the meat as I lifted him. He was as broadside as a plank. We might have caught him without the business of the Ferry. But he might have pulled out anyway.

About a possible safari: You will know by then whether Henny likes that sort of things. I should think Mary would but I always get in trouble when I tell someone to do something that is necessary. The politeness should be taken for granted. You can't always say, "Please Mrs. Jones take the leading beast if you would be so kind."

Or, "My dear Patrick the line from the port outrigger is falling and if you take it and release the drag, giving the fish an opportunity to get the bait well into his mouth, then if you cared to set the drag and strike smartly we might acquire an interesting specimen."

You, or rather I, am more liable to say, if we are looking toward the stern, "Take the right out rigger Mouse. Slack to him plenty and when you feel him running hit him hard."

Mary and I get along very well fishing. On a safari, if we had to have a white hunter, I would always have her hunt with the white hunter. I don't care about shooting anything special. There are two heads I still want; a Nyala and a Bongo. But they can both wait. I'd rather walk around with a gun and only shoot what we need for meat and especially I would like to wing shoot.

The last time we were in Africa we were always rushed trying for the different trophies and I would like to camp out this time staying in any good country and eat some of the wonderful things I remember and shoot some duck, snipe, francolin, lesser bustard and guineas and walk a lot. That is what we don't get here anymore with all the back country being built up so.

Sorry to bother you with such a long and worthless letter, Mouse. We had a wonderful Thanksgiving dinner last night after coming in from fishing.

Mary sends her love.

(.)

Papa

WOULD YOU MIND IF WE CAME TO SEE YOU

To PH, March 3, 1953
Finca Vigía, Cuba

Dear Mouse:

Philip wrote me about you buying a place in the Southern
Highlands of Tanganyika. We haven't heard from you since Henny
arrived. Mary had a very charming letter from Henny about
you buying the place and your travel but it had neither date nor
address and since my letters to Nairobi had gone unanswered she
has been waiting for an address to write Henny. Will give her this
last address I received today from Rice. Bum had written me for
your address and I have sent it to him today.

Mouse I wish you could take time and answer the questions I
wrote you in November about shipping stuff out, the best way to
get out without flying, how your car worked out and what model
and type it was and cost etc. It is now too late for us to come out to
Africa until after the Spring rains. Waited around figuring I would
hear from you, from Leland Hayward on the Old Man and Sea
picture deal. It has been set three times and each time they have
not come through. Really not their fault as Hollywood has been
thrown into a state of full panic by the switch or maybe switch, to
3 Dimensional pictures. But the way it has worked out technically
for me is that the deal is made and set. Then changed completely.
Then changed again. Leland Calls me to make reservations for

himself and wife and Spencer Tracy for a Friday, Sat, Sunday. On Tuesday he calls to have these reservations (almost impossible to get; cancelled). He has to fly to the coast. In the meantime other offers for the property lapse. Last Tuesday he calls and is back from the coast and everything is fine and he is writing fully. Today is Tuesday a week later and I have heard nothing. It has just been a winter out of my life that I can ill afford to spare and that I could have had a wonderful time with.

If you have time and feel like it would like to know what your place is like, where it is (to find on a map), what you figure on raising, if I can send you books or subscribe for magazines and to what permanent address, what magazines you miss and would like to have, in short, if you have time, or even taking time whether you have it or not write me answering the questions I asked first and these new ones?

What is the country like Schatz? What sort of shooting is there? Would you mind if we came to see you if we stayed at the local pub or camped somewhere and didn't bother you?

Philip wants us to come and stay at Machakos. We can always organize a couple of tents and live there the way we did the last time.

Did you ever get your hunt with Philip? He is very fond of you. Also can you give me the gen on when the good season is down where you are. I know in Kenya the grass is still high and it can be cold as hell in July. But if I am ever to get to Africa, or anywhere, I have to make some definite plans and not just hang around on other people's convenience and doing other peoples work.

Bum is fine. Had a good long letter from him day before yesterday. He was first in the very rough and dangerous course he took and now he is instructing it. The finish is the end of March and then they will all come down here for ten days. He is set up okay I think for regular army. I got letters from Dave Bruce, the Secretary of the Army etc.

Have trained hard with Mary for walking and shooting in Africa. Shot lots of snipe, quail and doves. Mary has shot very well. She had bad flu but is very well and happy now.

The other Sunday we went out in the stream and raised a good white marlin but he would only play with the bait. Later we caught some dolphin and they were so full of flying fish and sardines that they explained the marlin not being hungry. There have been no fish and no bait in the stream all winter and one norther after another in Florida although usually they would not break through to here. Lots of temperatures of 46 48 in Miami. Very bad tourist season everywhere.

No news of any sort from Gregory since his efforts on becoming of age.

Much love from Mary and me to you and Henny and good luck with the place. Aunt Sunny's husband died suddenly of Angina Pectoris leaving accident insurance. She stands to inherit a little from my Mother's estate but it cannot be terminated until all legatees, even technical legatees, sign the final release papers. So please send yours in promptly to the executor. Anything I receive under it will turn over to Sunny. You will see from Curry Harris's letter where the cash Mother inherited from me through my mother's estate went. Am trying to get Sunny straightened out. It is rough with the young boy to educate. But if I can write instead of handling chicken business all the time can carry any kind of weight they assign the horse.

Sure as hell would like to get away from this chicken stuff and see somebody like Philip before we are both dead as what do you call it and have you show me a new country and be cheerful and have some fun.

The only thing I do not want is to be yipped at by Gregory.

PAPA.

THE FARM WE HAVE BOUGHT

To EH, March 23, 1953
Dar es Salaam, Tanganyika (Tanzania)

Dear Papa

The farm we have bought is about fifty five miles south west of
Iringa, very near Sao Hill and just across the road from Southern
Highlands Club. Approximately 2,300 acres.

The altitude is just six thousand feet which at 8 degrees South
is equal in temperature to about seven thousand feet in Kenya. At
night it gets down to 55F in January, and you get one or two frosts
in July and August.

One rainy season beginning in November and lasting till April,
although only spotty rain in December and February. About forty
five inches in a normal year, but this year is dry all over East
Africa and they are going to have famine in the Northern Province.
Place would do best with fruits and vacaria, but transport so
expensive that pyrethrum is best possibility now. Will grow all
right along the river, where the ground holds enough moisture
through the dry season. There are some fruit trees planted already.
Citrus and pears seem to do the best. The pears are enormous like
those ones from the Northwest. Fruit trees growing now on the
farm are pears, peaches, plums, mulberry, guava, avocado, passion
fruit, and mango (this does not do so well at this altitude), also

apples. Coffee and tea will both grow but I don't think well enough
to do commercially.

Aside from small patches of virgin hardwoods there are quite a
few introduced trees planted. One beautiful high Eucalyptus with
a trunk two feet thick, wattle, a couple of avenues of silver mimosa
from Southern France, Australian flame trees, Mexican cyprus,
and even a few scatters pines (quite rare in East Africa). There are
two English generals buried on the place.

The house is built around court and except for the ceilings
is a nice place. Has a fire place in every room. The kitchen, after
being the home of native caretaker for three years, is really
indescribable. It would give Mary the horrors. The outside of the
house is covered in climbing roses which do very well. What it does
not have is one of those marvelous views which are so common out
here and which I wish very much it had. The native hardwoods,
however, are good. I have not seen anything like them anywhere
else in East Africa. They are real Green Mansion's trees with
straight high trunks and enormous crowns and beautiful delicate
undergrowth and soft, cushiony ground, and, of course, the two
English generals.

Since you have already made the trip though the Red Sea, I
would think you would enjoy the motor trip up from the Cape. It
is quite good road all the way, gas is about the same price it is in
the States when you have the benefit of the exchange. It is not in
any way comparable in difficulty with the trip from Kenya north to
the Mediterranean but like a trip out West like the roads were in
the '30s. For this trip the Buick station wagon would be absolutely
ok and I could let you have my truck for safari when you got up to
southern Tanganyka, for the Great North road goes by my farm.
Getting to the Cape is easy, for there are lots of steamship lines

and it is only a two weeks trip even by freighter, and I wouldn't be surprised if you could leave directly from Havana. A trip up from the cape by car would be fun. You would have fall weather if you arrived in April or May and dry weather all the way up. Stop over and see Jock the Bushworld country and Kruger National Park.

If you are at all interested, let me know and I will get the dope for you on where to stay and how much it would cost to get up here by car from the Cape. The route through Nyasaland is much more beautiful than the one through the Rhodesias.

Love to Mary & Finca

Much love
Mouse

WHAT SHOOTING IS THERE

To PH, April 10, 1953
Finca Vigía, Cuba

Excuse typewriter very stuck and needs cleaning.

Papa

Dear Mouse:

Thanks for your letter of March 23rd posted from Dar Es Salaam with the word about your farm and the fine coloured pictures. The letter from Nairobi never came. The last letter I had from you was from up country in Kenya before Henny came out. Philip wrote me about you buying the farm and I had held off writing to him and to you until I heard from you. This only to bring you up to date.

Bum is here now and he was delighted to read your letter and see the pictures. He had just finished instructing a course that ends with jumping and very tough problems in the mountains. He brought Puck and Muffet down. She is a delightful child and is very strong and getting to be awfully pretty. I heard her talk for three hours the other day and never heard her say I, me, or mine. She is quite a lot like Bum was when he was three. He had ten days leave before going back to instruct another eight week and then a twelve week course and is in the best all around shape I have seen him since he was out at the University of Montana. Puck very cheerful and fine and seemed to have a wonderful time here.

Spencer Tracy and Leland Hayward were here to do big business on Good Friday, Holy Saturday and Easter Sunday everything agreed on and Money to be deposited in N.Y. on Wednesday last. But today is Saturday and no monies deposited. Have a call in for Rice on the phone.

Probably not too sound for Mary and me to drive up from Joburg as we were planning to go out for a vacation and plenty of walking and that looks like a pretty long haul on the map. Is there any way to reach John's Corner from Mombassa, Tanga, Dar Es Salaam or Nairobi? All there is here is a Randand McNally Atlas. I want to see Philip very much and he suggested we come to him before going down to see your country.

Moose what shooting is there down where you are? Would appreciate it very much if you could tell me. Would there be any bird shooting in August, Sept. Oct.?

I know July is high grass and cold as hell in Kenya in July. I don't have anything particular that I want to shoot. We went to come and look things over and live healthy and have fun. Have been on this Island three years now and am over worked and stale. Get in good shape when we make a trip down to Paraiso. But when you get back everything is piled up; people are piled up; correspondence; have to grab the phone for Key West, for N.Y. for The Coast. Want to get away from all that. Want to freshen up and show Miss Mary some of the beautiful part of Africa. But not just ride through it in the dust or hauling out of mud holes. What we'd like would be see some Africa and have some un ambitious fun.

Book still goes well. It has settled to a steady sale of an average of 440 a week over the last nine weeks. Sold 60,000 in England (10 since January) goes like Mein Kampf in Germany; very well in France and Italy. It is in 50th some edition in

France and best selling book in Italy. Also good in the northern countries.

Sure as hell want to get a good change and vacation before I try to beat it with the next one. Can't do it. But I have to try.

Schatz what can we send out there? Can subscribe to any magazines Henny likes and any for you and have Scribners send out any books you want. Would you let me know what magazines you want. There are a few fairly readable books out. I can make a list and have Scribners ship them. Does stuff like that come through ok at your postoffice?

Our problem now is to get passage after the Coronation. Everything booked solid until then.

Is there anything you get a yen for that I can send out? Lee Samuels can always buy and ship from New York when he goes there.

Been standing by all morning waiting for New York call. No come. Had better send this now. What is your set up for radio or radio phono graph. Are you on battery?

Much love from here to you and to Henry. Mary, Bum, Puck and Muffet all send their love.

Papa

YOU MUST STAY HERE

To EH, June 17, 1953

John's Corner, Tanganyika Territory

British East Africa

Dear Papa,

I am sending a copy of this letter to Guaranty Trust in Paris in case you have already left Cuba.

Here is the gen on how to get here from Nairobi. By car, you take the great north road south through Arusha, Dodoma, and Iringa, turning off on the circle road to Mufindi about forty miles outside of Iringa on the way to Mbeya. When you have turned off at the Mufindi circle road you go a couple of miles to the Southern Highlands Club and they can tell you where our road is (it's only three miles from the club to our house). By plane, there is a regular service that leaves Nairobi every Tuesday at seven in the morning and gets to the Southern Highlands Club about three in the afternoon. The plane goes back to Nairobi on Thursdays. The fare round trip for two would be about two hundred and fifty dollars, rather expensive, I think. If you let me know, I can always come and pick you up, in Nairobi, or anywhere else. The roads will be dusty in August, but otherwise, very good month to travel, as you won't get rain anywhere. Will have two or three trips Organized here, and you must stay here as long as you like. We are a little short on furniture now, but we will have all that fixed by the time you get here. It is logical for you to see all the northern country first if you arrive in Nairobi, so don't think we will feel slighted if you don't come down here right away. We will expect you when you come. I will try and have some sort of outline of what we have to offer and send it to you care of Philip Percival. He can then advise you as to what it would be etc.

Congratulations on Pulitzer Prize. We will be very happy to see you and Mary. I think Mary will like East Africa, especially now that she is such a good rifle shot, also it is so beautiful to look at.

Much Love
Mouse

HAVING A FINE TRIP HERE

To PH, July 11, 1953
Pamplona, Spain

Dear Mouse:

Thanks for your letter with the gen on how to reach your farm.
We will arrive at Mombassa on Fernand de Lesseps Aug 27th and
proceed to Potha Machakos. Philip is going out with us and [EH
CANCELLATION: me] he will have another character to do the
work. Mayito is coming. He's very excited. We wont hit you until
late in Sept. I think will write you when Philip and I staff it out.
Am shipping guns etc, ammo etc out to Rees in Nairobi.

Having a fine trip here getting the gen for an appendix to
Death In The Afternoon on the evolution and decline of the modern
bull fight. One marvellous matador though Nino de la Palma's boy
Antonio Ordoez. Better than his father was on his father's best day.

Much love to you and Henny.

Papa

GOOD LUCK ON YOUR SAFARI

To EH, August 20, 1953
John's Corner, Tanganyika

Dear Papa and Mary,

Please forgive me for not being in Mombasa to meet. Mr. Percival
has written me your plans for first three weeks in Sept. and it
sounds very good. I think the country up there around Rift and
Masai reserve can't be beat anywhere. I think we can show you
some nice country down here, however, when you have finished
with the wonder places. The places I have in mind are the Buhoro
Flats (Wasangu) and the country between Iringa and Kilosa. On
the Flats I have shot sandrouse, guineas, and kwale and there is
rice and good wildfowl shooting, but now its too dry and we will
have to wait for the rains in November and December for the
wildfowl. As for game Eland, Topi, and zebra are common on the
open plain country, while sable, buffalo, and greater kudu are in
the thicker country around the edge of the flats and require more
careful hunting, and luck! If Mary wants a kudu, I think we can
get her one here, they are quite thick as kudus ever are. No rhino
that I know of, but Elephant hunting them more work than fun,
but there are big ones. As for hunting all game, it will be good
now up until the rains in November, with the game increasingly
concentrated around the permanent water. One advantage this
country have over Kenya and northern Tanganyika is that is it

quite well watered and you can take trips along the rivers, which is fun. If you could get a portable boat or canoe of some sort and bring it with you when you came, we could have a lot of fun with it.

There is also trout fishing. One place about fifteen miles from us. Very pretty and open little lake, filled with rainbows running about a pound and a half to two pounds. Down at Tukuyu, of course, there is the best trout fishing in East Africa, but that require a week's trip or so.

I've been very poor about writing lately, but please do write me what your plans are when you have finished your three weeks safari, as we do want to see you very much and, of course, show you our place and what hunting and fishing there is to be had in this region. It is now cold as hell here, but perfect in the hunting country, about a couple thousand feet lower.

Did you get my last letter, the one I sent a copy of to you care of the Guarantry Trust in Paris? I've heard nothing from you since April. I hope Baptista is not getting your mail. He seems to be having difficulties.

Good luck on your safari and hope to hear from you soon.

Much love,
Mouse

THE FOOD REMITTED IN PURGATORY

To PH, August 25, 1953
Machakos, Kenya

Dear Mouse:

Thanks very much for the letter you sent to the boat and to here. Missed the boat copy but got the carbon here. Had your other good letter too with directions on how to get down to your place and gen ed it out easily on the map.

I wrote you from Spain and from France. Spain could have been held up and undoubtedly the French postal strike which broke the day we sailed put the other out. If you didn't get the Spanish letter: we went to Pamplona, San Sebastian, Lecumberri, Madrid, and Valencia. I found you did not need a visa and knew Miss Mary would get in no trouble so took a chance and it turned out fine. The Prado was wonderful and the country and remaining old friends too. Saw eleven fights. Am bringing you a couple of those good leather cartridge carry paniers from Madrid. Got some good boots made there by my old boot maker.

Trip out as pleasant as the Union Castle can be. You get the food remitted in purgatory I think. Hope so.

Mr. Percival met us and we drove up here by Voi. Saw lots of game and birds.

Found a good camp up last night. Everybody speaks very fondly of you.

I'll write you the gen as we go along and as how things develop. Will see about rubber boats or canoes. Awfully sorry about your gun. Maybe we can get, with the number of the gun, a pair of barrels from Beretta. Gianfranco can find out.

Was terribly sorry to hear from Philip Percival that Henny was worried about her brother in Korea. If you will send me his name, rank and serial number I will cable the Adjutant General. The armistice was signed some time ago and he would have had to be listed as Missing; Believed Killed before that. If you give me the gen on him I will find out for her or tell her how to find out if she prefers to do it herself. We all hope he is o.k.

Excuse this worthless letter but feel sort of lethargic with the altitude and the long trip. Have to do some gen ing out with condition of Mayito unknown, Rees, the outfitter, quite ill and in bad shape but with everything fine that I have seen so far. I was so happy to see Mr. Percival at the boat after his bad siege of tick fever. I wish he had not come as it cannot help but be a strain on his health. But he stood the trip well and was feeling fine and cheerful today. We will try to help in every way on the Safari and not be a problem. The finest thing for me to do is to try to get in really good shape.

Country is dried up to hell everywhere in from the coast and the game not at all where it should be this time of year. The coast very green and for sixty miles inland. It rained very hard at Mombassa the night we got in.

Please give our love to Henny.

Hope her bro. is o.k.

Much love, Moose. Papa

This is Miss Mary's typewriter and I'm not so good on it.

THE HOUSE SEEMS MOST EMPTY NOW

To EH, November 13, 1953
John's Corner, Tanganyika

Dear Papa,

The house seems most empty now that you, Mary, and Mr. Percival have gone. I appreciated your coming down very very much, and I feel quite guilty about Mr. Percival. I hope you all had a more pleasant trip going back than they did coming down.

The cook turned out to be a marvel and the house head taken on a new tone even the cats are less hungry and look better groomed. Potha puppy has been in perfect health since that morning of the staggers, so it must just have been a bad hangover. He is a smart, loving, and very dog. G.D. sends you his best.

The rain has not yet come although it looks more and more like it every day. Now that the danger to the safari is over, I wish it would come, as things are now really too dry and the fire danger was very great. I have forwarded all your mail so far, but nothing that looks like your pictures yet.

The birds and impala have been delicious. We really must get the deep freeze as it would completely solve the next situation and we could also have fish, buying it in bulk and having it from up from Dar. Let me know if you see a kerosene deep freeze in Nairobi.

The books are wonderful, especially the goggle fishing one. Gig is supposedly sending me an aqualung, and if it comes in time we can have a great deal of fun at Mombasa with it, for there is a good reef, sheltered from the monsoon, and chuck full of crawfish. The only disadvantage is the enormous amount of sea urchins. I have never seen so many anywhere else. I am sure there must be bonefish, for there are ideal flats and channels for that.

Will send this letter now as nothing has really happened since you left but a series of good meals. Much love to Mary (she is really in wonderful shape), and very best regards to Mr. Percival and family.

Much love,
Mouse

THE ONLY BROTHER AMONG MY SONS

To PH, January 20, 1954
London, England

[HANDWRITTEN] New Stanley Hotel

Dearest Mouse:

Am so sorry about the laconic letters. Maybe been around too much with Ingleses. Christ knows us 'Kamba brag enough among ourselves. I enclose a letter I wrote Pop about the clinic. It gives details. Would you keep it for me, please, so I will have the true gen. Once you write it you can forget it. I dont know whether he was the one we ran into in the rain or not. That one was bigger and ranged from the swamp along the small river and up to my fiances shamba. He killed 10 goats there one night only eating one. He is a very bad boy and I hunted him 11 days including the use of the live goat. The goat would talk like hell all day but certainly knew how to keep his silence at night.

Mary was in bed with the curse when I found her lion. We went back and got her. Rough conditions for a mommy. Gin Crazed and I brought him to bay in a thick patch of bush about a mile N. NE. from where you killed your Granti. I got out and deployed taking the left flanks and tried to draw him. Mary in the center. G.C. on

– 211 –

the right. I was about 40 yards. He had a good chance to come but thought it over and negated. He started once but held it. Mary hit him behind a little. He gave us the old Kwanda and the fire fight started as it was nearly dark. I broke him down at 346 paces. G.C. hit me when he started to get up. G.C. missed him 6 times. I missed him 4. But things were a little rough. This is only to give you the straight gen. Miss Mary hit him twice, Arab Minor (mis spelled) says he is the father of Mayito's lion. Very beautiful and I think a little cowardly.

Miss Mary shooting good and beautifully. Shooting good like a surgeon. She got out of her slump. G.C. left me in charge of the area as acting ranger. Have 7 spears and have learned to spear good. 2 warthog, 1 hyena, 1 hunting dog, 3 jackal, etc. I hunted on foot at night without flashlight. Found the pack of hunting dog one night all asleep. You would love spear. It is sort of the poor man's goggle fishing. The trick is to go in and keep punching with it. You move as in boxing and keep on punching. Everytime you hit it is worse than a 30 06. The only bad part is that spears have degenerated and bend like butter. You have to [attach] a short blade spear on a shaft like a hoe handle. Charo who is an old man and a conservative character is sure I can kill faro. You only have to give it to him under the armpit. Please forgive not being English. You said you wanted the true gen. Killed 4 dog baboons with spear. One with only one through the chest. Another I hit the same place and he made an awful noise and bit and hit the spear so I withdrew spear, which was perfect I thought and start in fighting. The thing in Africa, nothing knows when it is dead. A rhino and a cow elephant with calf hit the water at the same time. The elephant broke the rhino's back and shoved a tusk up the left ass. I thought I saw a cow rhino being nursed by her calf.

Very early morning light with mist. OK. What it was in fact was Fisi (Biwana Fisi) hitting rhino in the genitals. Will show you the pictures on the coast.

We found 2 herds of buff. One 102 one 68 and I think Mary got lovely pictures. Also a rhino lay down and went to sleep and I went over and lay down too. It makes sort of a comic picture being a non picture rhino.

Schatz I'm terribly sorry you were ill. Dont give it any importance. Just take the stuff as prescribed. It is just something you get like the first time a man gets the clap.

I hope Henny is OK. Am sort of discouraged about that. But it is your Shauri and I never think about anything of you two except lovingly.

If you ever want a Kamba wife with the lovely insolence and good hard hands and other attributes I have two that you inherit by Droit de Segneur. I squared everything with Kalei [ILLEGIBLE] and it is as legal as anything illegal can be.

Shatz know I am not being Ingls nor locanic at all now but you were the only brother I had among my sons; Mr. Bumby admirable but not really intelligent and Mr. Gigi wonderful but always strange and then gone like a burned out fire cracker. Maybe he will come back. I hope so always. But I wish never to see him. Jimmy had a stroke and Bruce asked Gigi for money. He sent it but I have told Rice to return him all monies he sent. The local characters are trying to provoke the same old crisis. To try to get the place for nothing. I am prepared to fight this off indefinitely paying all costs myself. It is quite possible that after Mr. Braden spilling his ------- I may have to live in K.W. for a while. Will look after your stuff and send anything you want. The Cuba thing is really bad because I had to put peoples in the camp and now they know who did it.

About 4 are really dangerous. They have very short memories in Cuba. But the thing is rough as of now.

Mooser I dont know what other news.

For a while I had to do around the clock police work since the Game Dept. had definite role and Den was functioning in a richer area. Dick (le Prick) lost 14 assorted murderers M.M. MI KAMBA at Machakos maybe through jealousy. We didnt catch any but G.C. did a very good Shauri. He came down to organize our local defence and found Mr. Papa had a NKamba in every Shamba (Kwanda Na'Shamba tu) all roads blocked etc.

Tomorrow we leave with the N'Dege (Cessna 180) to go to the big lake and then to make an elephant survey on the Tana down to Lamu and then do the area up to the Juba. I wish you were with us. I have got back into flying like pulling on an old glove and have been down on the deck around 21 hrs. We are teaching G.C. to fly and I flew with him driving the bicho (with Roy helping) for 11/2 hrs through 1st class storms and rain. That Cessna does 180 MP hooked up and with the flaps down you can cut her down to 35 MpH and not stall. We do slow rolls down the main drag of Loitokitok after buzzing the Boma and cut the flag off with the prop. (Do not mention Men at work.)

Roy makes it so simple that Miss Mary (who is learning to love the deck) thinks it is simple. She wonders why Roy and I dont fly at 25 MPH and when it is necessary to pour the coal on fast she is convinced we are wasting money. We took the bicho into cyrrus cumulous for laughs and when it happened Miss Mary thought. "These gentlemen dont know how to fly."

OK Mr. Shatz. We will rendezvoy at KITANGA on JANUARY 30.

Dont be late. I would send you your trustee check and mine too but W'wendi has hidden all my monies and Kwenda Naka Shamba. Will deliver all checks.

Tried out 14 alleged Masai fighting bulls with cape and gourd. Not one worth a damn. Katei wanted to see a bullfight. Philip had told him about them. So I worked out all the stock they had between Kadgrado and Athi River. Used long gourd to slap on the ass etc instead of sword.

Much love Schatz. Send our love to Henny. Best regards to The Death Ranger. He is a good boy.

I love you always and am very proud of you.

Papa

SITTING ON HIS HAUNCHES

To EH, April 19, 1954
John's Corner, Tanganyika

Luganga Ju
Easter Monday, 1954

Dearest Papa,

What a lovely time we had at Shimoni, despite your being ill and me worrying about my place. Of course, when I got back everything was in perfect shape and I needn't have come back at all. Thank you very much for the fine time and the beauty boat.

I am all set to start the hunting season now, with Mumu, the old gunbearer who Mr. Percival got for me at Voi, and a new .375 Magnum bolt action that I bought in Moshi on my way back here. The rains have stopped a month early, which is bad for the country but good for the hunting as it will allow us to start a month too early. I am going out for four days day after tomorrow to scout a buffalo and a Kudu place, pick camps, and then come back and pick up Henny and tent etc.

Have had one day of duck hunting since came back from the Coast. Dr. Saska, the doctor you met in Iringa, and I went out to a water hole he knew and had an evening's shooting at knob nose ducks (a very large goose like duck, you probably know him). Very good. About four flights of a dozen or so birds each, and although I was shooting behind to begin with, I got three before it was too dark to shot. Mrs. Saska cooked them in an Hungarian way and they were delicious. Aside from that little trip, I have been home all the time. Have three good pictures done, and paint every morning. Also putting in the firebreaks. Have four boys working on it, and they seem to be doing quite nicely, about a fourth of the way done, and another month before the fire hazard starts. Place is looking very well now at the end of the rains. Had some very good sweet corn, which we ate for about four meals, and then a jackal broke into the garden fence and ate every ear that was left, just like Reynard the Fox, picking them off the stalk and eating them on the cobb, sitting on his haunches I suppose.

They are cracking down on firearms here in Tanganyika now. Two years prison for negligent loss of a firearm, but still no sign of trouble whatsoever. Don't think there will be, either, until they get a city like Nairobi.

Henny is in wonderful shape, has been ever since the Coast, and now she wants me to buy a boat. Perhaps one of these new twenty four foot aluminium cabin cruisers they are building in the States now might be feasible. At least no trouble with marine borers.

Magazine subscriptions you gave us have been marvelous. I especially enjoy the Field and Stream one.

Will write you about the hunting as it happens. Love to Mary.

> Much love, (.) (.) (.)
> Mouse

CHARGED AT ABOUT 25 YARDS

To EH, October 22, 1954
Nairobi, Kenya

Dear Papa,

Thank you very much for the check that you sent in your last
letter. I have done five big pictures and try and get photographs
of them to send you. After this last trip of mine in northern
Tanganyika I've decided I must buy camera, so I will use money
you sent to get one.

What a time, Papa! I got a really beautiful lion with a black
mane and fat as a pig, a nice onyx, a loverly lesser kudu with
the horns heavy and spread wide like the Greater Kudu, and a
buffalo with thick and heavy horns but falling off from old age.
Lost another buffalo which I'll describe in detail. Mumu and I got
up just before sun rise to walk over and have a look at a zebra we
had put out for lion about a quarter of a mile away from camp.
As we got close to the bait we saw there were three lionesses, two
immature males and about ten cubs on it. We got pretty close to
the bait when one of the lionesses spotted us and began to growl
and flick her tail. The cubs realized something was wrong and
scattered in all directions, two very small one toward us till they
were about 20 yards away. The three lionesses started walking
toward us with plenty of noise and we started backing backwards
slowly and when they caught up with the cubs they stopped and

we went back towards camp. On the way we saw two big old buffaloes just on the other side of a dry river bed about a hundred years away. Mumu had on a straw colored bushshirt and I think that was the cause of the trouble, together with the fact that there were many lions about as we had already seen and that these were two old bulls who had been kicked out of their herd and were therefore much more in danger of being attacked by lions. We crawled along the bottom of the river bed to the below the place where we had last seen the buffalo and climbed up the ten foot bank, Mumu in front and me just behind him with the bolt action .376 magnum with a bullet in the chamber, for I expected an easy shot at close range of an unsuspecting beast. As we reached the top one buffalo was all ready for us, having heard the noises of the grass and charged at about 25 yards. Mumu realized what was happening before I did, being in front and he jumped to the side, unfortunately without warning me. The first thing I saw was the front of the buffalo come out of the grass. I just had time to fire at his face (a body shot would have been useless to stop him at that distance: about six feet). He was not a wounded buffalo making that do or die attempt which I hope never to see but only a buffalo covering the retreat of his pal under the mistaken impression we were lions. At the shot, which hit him somewhere in the face, he threw his head up and I saw him shut his eyes and turn off to the right, just like the native cows wince and throw their heads when the herd boy comes at them with a stick. I slipt and fell and didn't get another chance for a shot until we saw him close at the heels of his pal about three hundred yards away going into the thicker cover on the hills along the river. We waited two hours and then followed the blood spoor until it gave out, but he kept going steadily away and never rested, for his pal kept him going, and we lost him for good in a burnt over patch which was covered with the tracks of a whole herd. It was a disgrace to lose him, but I don't think I did anything wrong in the whole hunt. I had to shoot and I only had time for a snap shot and was damned lucky it turned him. The buffalo was two days later in identical circumstances except that everything went as it should, I had an easy shot at about thirty yards which I put in the lungs instead of the heart. I didn't wait for him to stiffen up this time, for I was feeling awful about having to report two wounded buffalo, and we caught up with him in about twenty minutes and I broke his neck. I was very relieved.

The lion was a lucky business. We saw him while we were out scouting in the car about ten o'clock on an overcast morning. He was standing in a big clearing not even bothering to look at us, and I just got out of the car, walked toward him until I was close enough for a sure shot and knocked him over with the first show. He never moved, but I put one more shot in his shoulder when we walked up to him just to make sure. We skinned him out on the spot, rather than mess him up by taking him back in the landrover, and I have never seen such a fat animal. He was just like a stall fattened steer. When I went up to meet Henny, we took the skin out to Zimmerman, and saw your heads and skins, most of which are finished. That Gerenuk may have been diseased, but he certainly is a beauty, and the oryx of G.C. is fantastic.

Henny and I are both back now, with about four weeks to go until the rains, although they have already started up north. Kenya, as far as the settled portions are concerned is now a sinister place, crawling with troops and has lost that feeling of light hearted amateurism it has at the beginning. I didn't see a single cowboy. Anarchism is dead and now it is the Kikuyu versus the Others, and may the best man win. I got the feeling that they are going (both sides) to end up making each other into soap.

Much love to Mary and Finca.

Mouse

SENILITY ISN'T FUN FOR ANYBODY

To PH, July 22, 1955
Finca Vigía, Cuba

Dearest Mouse:

It was fine to hear about the big elephant and thanks so much for sending the cable. I answered to Percival's at Kitanga and hope you got it. Philip wrote me a letter with very high praise of you. I'll keep it for you. Mouse how is Philip? The speech he made at the White Hunter's Association meeting sounded very good. How is his cancer doing really and his back and the other troubles? I worry about him when I don't hear from him.

I enclose the check Rice sent me along with the accounting that went to you and Gig. Have endorsed it to you. You can pay Gig whatever share of it you and he agree on. I have taken no income from the property and have sent Rice's checks either to you or to him.

Mouse Gig has not written except to tell me of the negative results of the three short hunts he made with you in the rains. I had one letter before that saying he would like to get under way on his safaris a little faster and none since. I guess it is pretty hard to write him without antagonizing him although I tried very hard for a year or so but when he wants to shoot everything except dangerous game with a .220 Swift never having yet killed any of the big bullet eating antelopes that a 30 06 handles so well I have to write. Then he gets sore I suppose and gives me the silent treatment.

If it is ok could you let me know what his plans are and what he is doing. Also what his address is. Enclose a clipping about Douglas Aircraft which he advised me to invest money in. Since that advise it has lost 24% of its value while practically 75% of all other stocks have greatly advanced. This clipping, read carefully, will tell him why. It is still a nice stock to have bought in the years when I was writing For Whom the Bell Tolls and A Farewell To Arms and it will be even better if the DC8s turn out to not be like the Comets. But it would have ruined anybody who bought it heavily when Gig gave me the word on it. Just like if you were out with your .220 Swift in the Magadi country and in one of those one way tunnels through the high grass and the bush you ran onto a rhino or one of those old buff somebody had shooted before and spoiled his disposition.

What other news? Mary has to leave tomorrow to take her mother to a Christian Science rest home if her mother can travel from Gulfport. She has been staying in a very nice one there with a trained nurse and air conditioning and a room about as big as our living room at the Finca. But she quarrels with everyone and calls up all the time long distance to make complaints which she calls in the evening to deny having made. Senility isn't fun for anybody including the seniles I guess but a really mean senile can make quite a lot of trouble. I think the biggest old buff we kill and possibly some elephant are mean seniles but am anxious to get back to Africa and investigate this further.

Meantime Miss Mary's mother has discovered for really the

long distance telephone. If your shares of ATT have risen lay it to that. She says that it costs nothing and calls in a day several large cities where she has old friends.

Have been working hard every day I don't have to interrupt it and am on page 506. It is a pretty good book I think. Back doing much much better than any body figured and liver and kidneys too. Head works o.k. Left eye and left ear not so hot but am sure shooting the .577 would probably clear the ear out good.

Bum sounds fine and will be as long as the market stays up. Am pretty sure that he has some sort of escape route figured out when the break comes but hope they won't cut him off at Eagle Pass.

Stocks fell slightly under a report of "A Peace Scare" at Geneva.

Please write Moose. I will try to write funnier letters. Yest was birthday and laid off work today to write you in my fifty sixth year. Shit maru how the years go. But we have good fun and that is more than most people have and we can both shoot in the clutch too. I'm bragging. I mean you can and I could and will again.

Mary sends best love. Please give our love to Henny and to Gigi if he is still around. I take it from your letter that he solved that difficult decision of whether to go back and do the work he should do or stay around and hunt in July which he had decided was the best month of the year to hunt. If you had big rains get out the double length step ladder. July is the month. Might be very good though in some of that dry bush fly country if you can work out the water.

We have to do actual fishing photography on the picture first two weeks of September. So far no current in the gulf but the water, yesterday, was beautiful and the current might start with this new moon. Have all the old time fishermen of Cojimar hired.

If no fish then will do last of April 2 weeks and first two of May at Cabo Blanco. There the thousand pound marlin is like the grunt. They feed on 40 to 100 pound squid and they catch them in 45 minutes belly up. I'd like to get a real fish here. Will let you know how things go. And try to get to Africa between the two.

Best love Papa
(Küss)

YOU WRITE SO STRAIGHT AND GOOD

To PH, August 24, 1955
Finca Vigía, Cuba

Dear Mouse:

Thanks for letter mailed MBULU Aug. 15 which arrived today.
Mary also had a letter from Henny. Hope Safari goes well and
that you like Russell Douglas and visa versa I figure anybody
who doesn't like Mr. Percival, Mister Bum, you or me is a fool.
I think Mr. P. would agree if he knew Mr. Bum. He might have
reservations on me but not on you.

Here starting next Thursday we make small oceanic safari
for fishing for OldManetc. hereafter referred to as TOMATS ie
The Old Man etc. Have four boats fishing (cojimar old style boats
fishing 4 lines each) and Mayito's TENSI (fast) and Pilar riding
herd on them with a four thousand dollar combat camera with
three telescopics and a cinerama camera or maybe just super wide
screen in each boat. After 5.30 till dark. Afterwards juntas etc. It
is only for 15 days but is like 2 six day bike races plus three days
extra. Very classy kraut camera man named Hans Hoenekamp.
The mains get in tonight at midnight. The balance of unit on the
29th. Boat hooking fish fires signal pistol; bull talkers etc.; boat
to boat Trying to keep it simple, simple but always problems. Two
hurricanes so far and one building but current very strong and

dark and plenty fish down deep. Wish the fish were under contract but neither are the animals except at Carr Hartley's.

I hope you will be a fine White Hunter if that is what you want to do but if you only want it for experience will understand.

Is there any way I can ascertain without putting M5 on him whether Gig is going to resume his medical studies or what his plans are? Am glad to hear you think Africa is doing him good. Would advise him to write me if certain things mean anything to him.

Have been working hard and putting all the shitty interruptions in different packages in my head so I could work. Instead of packages I guess compartments is better. You wrote wonderfully about the lioness teaching the cubs to kill. Thanks very much. I love your letters and you always write so straight and good about Africa. Had a good letter from Den yesterday with late gen on Mayito. When you get back to Arusha better get in touch with Den as he was talking about going down to Mayito to see you and also had some very bad lions lined up for you guys in October at Koora where he had to take out 7 control lions by himself in five acres of long grass. Wizard ops in prospect. I would give anything if I could make it too. Maybe I can.

Best love to Henny and to you and best to Gigi and his family. Mayito's address is Care Barclay's Bank, Nairobi. Den's is Game Ranger, Kadjiado, Kenay. Mine, unfortunately is still the Finca.

Mary sends much love.

Papa

HAVE AT LAST MANAGED IT

To EH, September 9, 1955
Ngorongoro, Tanganyika

[HANDWRITTEN ON AIR MAIL STATIONERY]

Dear Papa,

The last three months have been very hectic for me, as I have
been trying to break into the hunting business, and have at last
managed it. I don't recommend it, but I decided it was the only way
I could get to really know the whole country under the different
conditions of weather and get practice with the different animals.
As soon as I really begin to know something, I will try for a job
with the game department or national parks.

I saw Mayito in Arusha last week, and he is in very good shape
after getting a better sable than his last trip and also a good kudu.

Henny saw Denis in Arusha just before I got back and he
told her about the lions. I don't think I will be able to make it but
Mayito will and also Gig. I wish I could tell you more about Gig's
plans, but they change each time I see him. I will try and find out
more when I am back in Arusha between the 12th & 15th.

I hope you are having good luck with T.O.M.A.T.S. Mayito was
worried about rough sea and too much rolling of cameras, but
rough sea is when you catch the fish, isn't it?

Ngorongoro is really lovely this time of year. I am taking some people out for lion pictures and we got some beauties this morning of two lions in love. Good specimens and perfect light from 8:00 am to 11:00 am with colour fine six inch lens and close ups of actual mating at about 25 years. Lion is pretty good, can make love over ten times in one hours. People fully satisfied.

Will write again soon.

Much love to you and Mary,

Mouse

WE ARE ALL STINK PROUD OF YOU

To PH, October 12, 1955
Finca Vigía, Cuba

Dear Mouse:

Thanks very much for your fine letter and for taking the time to
write it when you are so busy. We are all very proud of you and
happy that you are doing what you want to do and doing it well.
My money was always on you but especially since you turned up so
fast at Entebbe with the indispensable Shillingi. Good old Mouse.

We did what was necessary and could be done with TOMATS
preliminary shooting but I always knew we would have to go to
Cabo Blanco short of a miracle and we didn't draw any miracles.
Had Geo. down to train me and handle me and was able to go 8
and ten hours steering on the flying bridge without going down.
Would soak caps in salt water and then at noon put on old African
hat well soaked. We had parts of 3 hurricanes and eight days
straight had to tow the Cojimar boats in with real line squalls.
The photographic work was very interesting but difficult as
Cinemascope cameras mounted almost at water line in the stern
so you had to maneuver in high seas to point the ass of boat at
the small boat and fish rather than the bow which is easy. The
technicians were pleased with how we did it and I think we did it
as well as we could. Elicin was very good and we worked together
fine with the two boats and got fine film of marlin up to 477 and

many necessary galano and mako shots as well as schools of
dolphin. I held one school in beautiful light and dark purple water
in camera range for 55 minutes while taking nine fish from it.
Some of the circling and lazy eights for four five hours at a time
is exhausting and etc. But it was sort of like the war or hunting
when the thing happens and we were never more than 4 seconds
in getting onto range of a boat with a strike. Used flare pistols for
signals. You would have enjoyed it and I most certainly could have
used you.

My ambition is now to hunt with Mousie as my White Hunter.
I will say, "Take him, Mouse. The very sight of him terrifies me."
My other ambition is to hunt Gig just once in Magadi.

If you have any gen on his plans let me know. I wrote him a
couple of letters to the New Arusha Hotel but no hear.

Bum is down here for two weeks. Sends his love. His weight is
a little high and some sun and exercise will do him good. He has
some plan for his investment service which takes in Latin America
starting with Cuba. The hell of investment services is that next
year come this time they will probably be boiling mutation mink
stoles and two ton Cadillacs to try to make a nourishing soup. As
Lewis F. Wolfson said, "There will never be any lack of prosperity
so long as the menace of Communist aggression can be preserved."
This in not an exact quote. Must knock off and swim with Bum. He
will write something to put in this. We are all stink proud of you
and plan to move wherever you move and place ourselves under
your protection. (To be continued.)

Mr. Bumby has written his message so will close this now and
get it off. Much love and love to Henny. Best to Gig and his wife
if they are still there. Bum and I are so stink jealous of him being
able to shoot, not have to work, not have to study, not have to jump

out of aircrafts nor ever fight, not have to support a family, nor
relatives nor ever give a presny and be out hunting now in Oct.
when his old man and his older bro. still have to work and eat
merde that I doubt if he would get many votes for sheriff until he
has killed an armed man who is seeking to kill him. There is one
word for his life so far which is, in Spanish, aprovechar. Pues que
sigan aprovechando hasta que viene el bicho. Sometimes I wonder
if he lists Mother and Ada in his Game Book under Manamouki
(pas trouve).

Must pause to let comprehension and appreciation juvenile
delinquents seep back in to the well and banish envy which we
all know is a sin although I wish it were the worst I have ever
committed. Bum and I are having a fine time and hope he is too.
He is as fine a boy as ever Mouse and at thirty two he is tired of
being conned and he doesn't want to con anybody else. He loves to
shoot now and shoots very well.

Mooser, never get too tied up. A man should be tied only by the
basic ground rules and his own conscience.

Please let me know anything I can do and again send love to
you and Henny and any other Hemingsteins whose papers are in
order.

Papa.

A VERY EXCITING RHINO HUNT

To EH, March 26, 1956
Arusha, Tanganyika

Dearest Papa,

I have just got back from three weeks at Johns Corner. Place was
in good shape. They had kept it from being overgrown in the rains,
which have been very heavy this year. I think the firebreaks since
that bad burning the year you came have done some good as far
as the francolin are concerned. I had good bird shooting with Kali
all over the property. A species called Red Winged francolin. They
look very much like a hen pheasant, with no bare spot on the
throat, and the primaries of wing are the same reddish brown as
those of a peacock. I wish I knew more about their feeding habits,
and whether it would be feasible to rear them like pheasants or
bobwhites, for they are an excellent bird to work with dogs. Except
when pairing off to breed, they live in covies of a little more or less
than ten and hold even better than bobwhites. When Kali makes
a point, I can go in and kick them up almost one by one. They
always flush with a loud screaming cackle which adds a lot to them
as a game bird. I wish knew more about feeding habits, breeding
season, importance of grass fires, and predators (hawks and jackals
especially).

We are leaving for Turkey next week and get back to
Tanganyika the end of May. Will write what it is like.

Last safari was very hard work because of the rains. There was no break of dry weather in February as there should be in a normal year. We did have a very exciting Rhino hunt in the forest on Lemagrut just outside the Serengeti park. There is a sector of country left out of the Park that runs from Endulen right up to the top of the mountain, which is over ten thousand feet. At about seven thousand feet there is a peculiar forest made up of only one kind of high altitude flat top thorn tree with a lot non thorny bush growing underneath. We tracked two mornings in a row and got our shots both under 15 yards, Very lucky with no trouble, but it is a tricky place. One of our hunters, Anton Allen went up there last week, and although he got a thirty two incher for his client, had to shoot two other Rhino in self defense which did not go over too well with the Game Department. Papa, you would enjoy that little sector of forest. The trick is to see how far you can walk without shooting a Rhino. You are very popular with the local inhabitants, because it is dangerous for the children to walk any distance from the actual shamba because of the rhino and they are always killing Cows that stray into the forest.

Please write us what it is like in Peru. Very best of luck in getting a big fish.

Much love,
Mouse

GAME GOING AT A TERRIBLE RATE

To EH, August 18, 1956 (age 28)

Arusha, Tanganyika

Dear Papa:

Thank you very much for your letter. I know what a strain the picture people must have been.

Have been working since June, and just got my full license yesterday, after a year's apprenticeship with a very good if somewhat stingy teacher. I got much more than I deserved, for Jerry Swynnerton made me an honorary game ranger at the same time he gave me my license, which was a very kind thing for him to do indeed. It all makes me a little bit uneasy, as it is so easy to make a mistake and then you go down just as quick as you came up.

Last trip, for the month of July (I missed your birthday because there was no near post office) was in south western Tanganyika, well south of Tabora, and I can now give a pretty good answer to anyone who is of the opinion that there is nothing worth shooting in Africa south of Kondoa Irangi. It is a very good area, Papa, offering every type of country, good mained lions, big elephant, the plentiful and almost tame buffalo of the past, good roan, sable, and greater kudu. Only rhino are scarce, but they do exist. In thirty days we got good specimens of everything but rhino, but the best part of the trip for me were two hunts, one for a wounded roan, and the other for Puku in lake Rukwa. On the first, we saw a herd of roan late in the morning on the edge of an mbuga:

[HAND-DRAWN MAP]

We tried and failed to get a shot before lunch, so we stopped and had lunch on the edge of the mbuga, in plain sight of the herd of Roan grazing out in the long grass. They lay down in the heat of the day and got up again just as we finished our nap about three forty five in the afternoon. We tried stalking them again, and the client had to take a long shot at the only male, breaking his left foreleg right where it joined the body. We followed him up quickly and I shot him again with 450/400 and he went down suddenly like a typical spine shot, but in about thirty seconds he was up again and in with the females into the trees before we could get a clear shot. It was now about four thirty and we had some delay in finally picking up the blood spoor, but once we had it, it was pretty easy to follow and he was keeping well ahead of us. We bumped into a couple of buffalo after about a half hours tracking, and this held us up considerably, for the trackers lost the blood spoor in the excitement. Got the blood spoor again and followed it until too dark, when we blazed a tree. We got an elephant the next morning (68 pounder), and so did not get back to our blaze until about four thirty the next evening. Followed the dry blood spoor for half an hour until we came to where he had laid during the night and morning and where he had emptied his bowels. I knew we would get him then, and we did flush him very shortly. After he was dead, I saw where my original shot had missed his spine by less than an inch. It was hard on him, poor beast, but a very good job of tracking to get him on an old spoor like that.

The Puku shoot was courtesy of the Red Locust people in South Rukwa. All young south africans with one english scientist, and they run their whole locust area as a game preserve, with an occasional permit given to shoot puku because they can't be obtained anywhere else in Tanganyika except in the Kilombero. Very exciting hunt which finally ended up with our having to take all our clothes off and swim a river to finish off the puku.

Henny is very well, and we have a very nice apartment for hunting season in Arusha. She is really very patient and good with me. Gig is in good shape and working hard at his farm, but I think he has chosen a very expensive way to find out about farming, its pros and cons.

You must come back to Africa soon, as the game is going at a terrible rate.

Please give my love to Mary and remember me to all our friends. Henny sends love.

much love,
Mouse

IT IS LONELY HERE NOW

To PH, September 28, 1956
San Lorenzo del Escorial, Spain
Hotel Felipe II

Dear Mouse:

It is lonely here now. Fine fall days with the high sky of the Meseta 32 minutes into town with the Lancia Gianfranco sent from Udine. Very good driver. Saw two good bull fights on the way down at Logrono. On Oct 12 we go to Zaragossa for 4. Then back here to put in time on Miss Mary's anemia. She seems better and has a fine appetite. Will have good partridge shooting here. Can fire as many shells as at doves in Cuba. Starts Oct 14.

Am in fair shape and will try to practice a little shooting first. Antonio Ordonez (matador) has a friend with a finca about 15 minutes from here with a lake with bass and some ducks and bitzkies and walk up partridges. Wish I had my own guns. But Denis is taking care of them now at Kadjiado.

Not much news except how lovely the country is and how nice people are to us. They dedicated 2 bulls to us at Logrono and the crowd cheered. Cesar Giron did a wonderful faena on his and killed well and Joselito Huerta, a Mexican, did things you could not believe and cut both ears, the tail and a foot.

Antonio, if he gets a good bull at Zaragossa is going to dedicate it and put in short banderellas (when you break them in half) and kill recibiendo. Wish you could be there. You sweat it out. But it is wonderful with a great fighter. I sweat it out too much.

You're probably out but am waiting for a call I put through to the Finca and was lonesome waiting so wrote to you.

Much love to you both.

Papa.

GOOD CHANCE LAST TRIP FOR ME

To PH, October 26, 1956
Finca Vigía, Cuba

Dear Mouse:

Haven't heard from you since wrote from N.Y. I think. But Mary
had a very good funny letter from Henny.

Since then we have booked passaged on the "Africa" leaving
Venezia Jan 2 arriving Mombassa Jan 14. Dennis has my guns in
the armoury at Kajiado and will ship out 3 additional guns from
Abercrombies and ammo for everything. The question is where
to and who to have organize a 6 week safari? Have written Mr.
Percival and Den for advice and am writing you.

There will be Mary, me, Antonio Ordonez (who has turned out
to be a great great bull fighter and cannot sleep for wanting to
get out. He has 12 fights in Mexico and S.A. first and plans to hit
Nairobi between Jan 20–25) and maybe Mayito. Must cable Mayito
when finish this letter. I would like to get our old boys and hunt
at Salengai, Kimane, and maybe Magadi if we can would love to
hunt with you if we can or have you as a white Hunter with us
if possible.

Please write what are possibilities could you meet us at
Nairobi and set it up and make some money for you and your firm.
With Den and I and Mayito, Antonio and Mary we could have

some fun. Antonio is working hard on Swahili and his wife says he wakes her up in the middle of the night talking it.

We are in hands of Doctors getting fit for trip. Good chance last trip for me but have fooled doctors before. If cant hunt uphill will hunt on the level want to have fun.

Have written Philip about trying to locate the old mob. If they are working for someone else maybe you could take leave and join us as a White Hunter. Maybe you can organize it with your people. Think it out consult Den and Philip and let me know.

Love to Henny.

Gig went to Finca stayed 2 weeks. Drank up everything even awful samples given us by curo Minoz that I only kept for sick cows. But was never drunk and [ILLEGIBLE] all the time. Rene said Gig wrote very nice and loving letter which Roberto forwarded. Nobody can blame him for what the Public Relations officer of army did to him. But on other hand he hasnt quite made The Quiet Birdmen yet.

Bum in N.Y. on training course with Merril Lynch Pierce, Benner etc. He's doing well. Puck acting up pretty bad. This word from old Bum himself. Will give you all family Real Property etc. gen when I see you.

Miss Mary sends love.

Much love
Papa

MUCH MORE FUN THAN SHOOTING THEM

To EH, November 6, 1956
Arusha, Tanganyika

Dear Papa,

Both Henny and I are very excited to hear that you are planning
to come out the end of January. As you may have guessed, all this
Suez trouble has not done the Safari business any good, and I
have not been out with a party since the end of Prince Bernhard's
trip in the middle of October. I am tentatively booked to go out
with the son of a big boot polish manufacturer from Genoa in
January, and if it comes through, I don't think I can afford to turn
it down, as work is not that easy to get now, which means that I
would probably not be free to meet you in Mombasa at the end
of January. However, with the Suez trouble, your plans may not
turn out exactly as you have arranged, and we may be able to
work something. I am keeping in touch with Den and Mr. Percival,
and something good should come out of it. February is a very
good month both for southern Kenya and northern Tanganyika,
although not good for southern Tanganyika, which is a pity, for
there is some very nice country down there that I would have liked
to have shown you.

I had some very nice hunts on my last trip, down on the Bubu
river in Central Province for Elephant (we didn't get one), and
around Longido Mountain, for Gerenuk. I never hunted with

the Prince, only with his a.d.c. Geertsea, who is the head of the game court of Holland and the Prince's doctor, a very difficult and tempremental client. He would begin to shake with very bad buck fever just before he shot, still, I was very pleased when he managed to get a fifteen and 3/4 inch Gerenuk with me.

Henny is in wonderful shape and very pleased with her flat here in Arusha. She doesn't mind my being out of work for a month!

I am having a very good time now with maps (1/125,000) and various papers on the vegetation and fauna of the Territory. Because of the Tsetse fly, the two things have been very well studied in this country. Some of the work on Greater Kudu is lovely: everything about their habits and food. It is really much more fun than shooting them. I have a very good game camera know, with a stock and trigger just like a gun, and a turret so I can use three lenses.

Please keep me up to date on your plans, and I will also keep in touch with Den and Mr. P.

Much love to you both. Henny sends love.

Mouse

LIKE KING-SIZE BEES

To PH, November 14, 1956
San Lorenzo de El Escorial, Spain

Dear Moose:

Here is the latest gen: Talked to Lloyd Trestino last night. The
canal has to be considered blocked. The Africa will leave Venice on
Jan 2. It was due Mombassa the 14th. Now will round the Cape
and reach Beira (Mozambique) on 25th or 26th. May continue to
Mombassa. May have a shuttle service or another ship Beira to
Mombassa. We would figure to be Mombassa by Jan 30th at latest.

If you can hunt with us for 6 weeks had no idea of getting it
on the cuff. Want to pay you your full price and thus keep dough
more or less in the family. Den suggested this too. He is going to
take leave to hunt with us. That makes one white hunter, 1 game
ranger, 1 Honorary Game Warden (Kenya) which ought to hold us.
We will be 3 people Mary, me and Antonio Ordonez.

We want to have fun, are after no special great heads, would
like to shoot the beasts that run both ways after we shoot in on the
meat beasts.

Philip said he would round up our old boys. But was doing
it through Safari land. Den wrote he could rent an outfit. Philip
said to ship guns, ammo from NY. to Safariland. I wrote Den to
tell Safariland we would pay for all services and for him and you
to coordinate with Philip what we should do and write me and

cable to whom ship guns, ammo. My own guns are in armoury at Kajiado. Den said he would meet us at Mombassa and we could base with him in Kajiado while we hooked up with you and decided where to go.

Please give this gen to Den and Philip. Would be glad to pay you double what the shoe shine king would.

I offered to get a new big Land Rover in London and bring it out. Could bring it in AAA and then pay duty on it and leave it out there. Den thought might be sounder financially to buy 2nd hand Rover in Nairobi and then re sell. I am not up to date on Transport situation as of now.

Having to tran ship at Beira (if necessary) could make a problem.

Anyway that is the gen so far. Have a good 6.5 fixed to Mary's measure which may help her problem with the old gun. Have Swedish 30 06 they gave me Husquana and Mr. Thompson's 30 06 to be air expressed out by Abercrombie. Also 20 gauge shotgun for Mary with ammo and ammo for all rifles and .22's.

Write me to Guaranty Paris or cable Guarritus Paris anything you want or need.

Have had some wonderful driven partridge shooting. They pour at you down a draw or over a steep small hill like King size bees. Will bring some pictures.

Better close and get this off. Please co ordinate with Den on the boys, (would mean a lot to me to be with my Kamba brothers instead of strangers we know each other pretty well).

Mary is better all the time. I've got this one trip in me I figure. Am not running as a hypochondriac. Am on very strict and boring regime and the sea voyage, swimming etc will be good for me. Aircraft not so good. (For me I mean. Love them same as ever.)

Best love to Henny. News on Gig. He wrote fine letter from Finca. Hasn't sent any Army address yet but hear is at Fort Jackson, [SC] (paratroop) Jane married 5 days after divorce. That sounds like a Cunningham combat camera you have. Very good.

Much love
Papa
(.)

THE BEASTS THAT RUN BOTH WAYS

To EH, November 21, 1956
Arusha, Tanganyika

Dear Papa,

I have just been up to see Denis. We talked everything over and this is what we have planned. Safariland is out, if that is ok by you. I will see that they are treated with courtesy, but you are under no obligation to them. They are a no good outfit and just about to fold. You will do much better with our firm, and it will cost you less. The price for you, Mary, Antonio, Denis, and myself as hunter will be:

Shs 27,997/32 for 42 days (roughly $4,000.)

Shs 666/66 for each additional day over 42

milage: 50miles a day, over that, Shs 2/ per mile

Transport will be one brand new long wheel base landrover with hunting car body and one five ton Bedford truck. Denis will bring his own landrover and will only ask for petrol and oil. Don't bother to bring out any vehicle. Tentage, equipement, boys, and food will be first rate, exactly the same standard we supplied Prince Bernhard in September. I will be personally responsible for every detail of running the safari and my boss has promised me you will get the pick of everything.

Denis and I will meet you in Mombasa or any other East African port and your safari will start from the day you leave Arusha and the day you get back there. confirming the price I have given you and giving approximate dates. Starting date is important. If it doesn't matter to you, send the usual 25 per cent deposit (About $1,000.00) and I will see that you get it back at once, if you do have to cancel. It is good for my face, however, for you to make the deposit if you do really hope to come.

Papa, you don't know how really happy I will be to take you all out if we can manage it. Don't worry about the hunting, we will have plenty of the beasts that run both ways. Will write more about that later on, but want to get this off to you now and get to bed.

Much love,
Mouse
(.) (.) (.)

P.S. Keti, choro, & your gun bearer most welcome & appreciated

IT IS A DULL FIGHT

To PH, December 15, 1956
Finca Vigía, Cuba

c/o Guaranty Trust Co. of N.Y.
4 Place de la Concorde
Paris

Dear Mouse:

You must know what a disappointment it was not to get out to see
you and Henny and Den and to make a good safari with you. So
will skip it. Couldnt be worse for me.

Here is how it worked: we took Mary to Spain and fixed up for
all practical purposes her anemia and a spasmodic enteritis and
colitis. She feels fine now and had a good blood count 4,030,000 a
little low but sound and is over the lassitude and the symptoms of
bad anemia. Will keep on building her up.

Dr. Madinaveitia found my blood pressure very high 200
over 210 I went on very severe diet and almost no liquids and got
down to under 200 lbs. But the pressure wouldnt come down and
he found an inflammation of the aorta, which evidently picked up
working hard on those oversized fish and holding them so close
for pictures. High blood pressure could blow this, he said and if I
could stick with diet, regime etc. could bring pressure down and

everything would straighten out and be sound. He thought I could do this on the sea voyage out.

Then came loss of canal (Suez not alimentary) and the Jan 2 ship would not arrive at Beira (as far as it would go and no connection) until Jan 23 25. That meant we couldnt get going on Safari until Feb. But would still have come out except that in spite of most rigorous diet, regime etc. blood pressure stayed around [EH CANCELLATION: around 19] after going down to 180 over 80 went back up to 200 over 105. No good and I had to cable cancelling.

Have worked on it like a son of a bitch 1 piece of dry toast for breakfast cup of tea, drink not more than a glass of water grilled meat, salad and fruit 1 glass of wine with a meal (In Spain and France) a little whisky and water; not supposed to make love while the artery healed and finally and finally got down 195 over 105 180 over 100 and now 170 over 95. So am winning. But is a dull fight. They finally traced it to cholesterol forming in the arteries and now have very good stuff to combat that and should be fit in 3 or 4 months. Then can ease back to normal on everything. Will keep in good touch and give you plenty of warning when can come out next year. Hope for Sept. and stay a decent length of time.

Get this off to give you the gen.

Let me know what I owe on any expenditures or cancellations you made and will send check.

Please forgive Hypo chrondriac sounding letter. Did not even go to Dr. Felt fine. He just said when I casually asked him about having nosebleeds at Escorial "Let me have a look at you."

Probably was a good thing to check though.

Much love old Mouser. Had so many damned things to talk to you about.

Merry Christmas to you both. Mary sends her best love and is writing Henny.

I feel awfully bad about not getting out. Much worse than I care to write. But I guess you know about that. Will make a good fight on this one like on all the others.

Boisey and Blackie have both died so my flanks are a little open. Leave here Jan 23rd.

Papa.
(.) (.) (.)

BEST HUNTING IS TRACKING

To EH, December 23, 1956
Arusha, Tanganyika

Dear Papa,

We are very much disappointed that you and Mary will not be able to come out. I hope that all the mix up about Safarilands, boys, and so forth did not help to make it impossible. If you do want to come out some other time, let me know and I can make the arrangements for you. I was a bit of a shrinking violet this time because I very much wished to avoid hurting anyones feelings, but I can and will give you the best hunting you can get in East Africa, and if I am lucky enough to have my own outfit by then, you will get it at cost. But one thing we can both comfort ourselves with is that it is the smell you get when you blow out the barrels of a shotgun that is just as nice as when the fleeing lion gets the hired help's bullet up his ass. The best hunting I have had, and I've had considerable in the last two years, has been tracking. The most interesting animal to track is the elephant and that is why he is about the only sporting animal left in Africa. You wrote once in an article comparing the sea and elephant hunting that the elephant only got so big and you never knew what you might get in the sea. It was not a valid comparison, because the tusks of an elephant are always a mystery until you see them (like when a big fish Jumps) and they can be any size, the largest this year is a hundred and

eighty a side from south western Tanganyika. If you are shooting
on a Tanganyika residents license that elephant is worth over a
thousand bucks after deducting the license fees. If you hunt them
in thick cover, where the big ones spend most of their time, it is
very exciting, because so much of it is by ear. You are closing up on
a good track and all at once there is a loud crashing noise in the
thicket ahead that means an elephant has got your wind and is off.
I've run in to have a quick look and run back just as quick when I
saw the little calf like a pig between its mothers legs. But the most
exciting time I've had is crouching and then running like hell when
a wall of twelve bulls all shoulder to shoulder come charging (the
word is really appropriate here, it is just like Hannibals elephants)
down your wind. You make it to a piece of high ground and sit
listening to them as they cut back and forth over your tracks like
bird dogs screaming and grumbling with fright and hate. Then
they work up their courage and make a break from the thicket
across about a hundred yards of clearing, just like a war fleet
making a dash down a channel to the open sea. And they make it
to a sea of thicket a hundred miles long without a break.

> Much love to you both,
> Mouse

JIMMY HAD A FINE TIME WITH YOU

To PH, April 11, 1957
Finca Vigía, Cuba

Dear Moose:

Thanks for the two fine registered letters. Just finished writing Jimmy Robinson to thank him for everything

Jimmy had written me he was sending you a pair of good glasses. Hope they arrive o.k. He had a fine time with you Mouse and has really gone to bat all the way. From all I hear you are getting excellent word of mouth recommendations too. Am getting to the point of discouraging known shits who would like to hunt with you. Tell me if this is wrong I thought Jimmy would be down your alley though and that you would like him. He has so many friends who trust his recommendations and he is very valuable to have backing you. You tell me how you want me to act about everything. Have tried to be an absolute non interferer. But it is stupid for me not to steer ok people to you when I know your ability and worth.

Bum is here with his two children and Puck. His address is Edificio RIOMAR MIRAMAR Havana Cuba. That is a very nice apartment just across the Almendares River mouth from the Vedado Tennis Club. New since you were here. It isn't expensive as they have it under good terms. But living is very expensive. Puck is homesick for Twin or maybe Portland. Bum is working hard. He is an angel with the kids.

If you'd rather I did not write about Gig can skip it. Certainly it doesn't do any good. The barest gen on him is this. The Greek took him for all his money no matter what you hear from him or anyone else. I flew him out there fast with a possible salvage plan and cash to retain a good lawyer. He writes he is salvaging $25,000 pounds out of 40,000. Actually he is getting 2,000 pounds and the rest is to be payed back over a period of years. His conceit makes him as confident that he will get this as it made him confident that he would make the millions he wrote me about when the Greek conned him originally. I went over the Greek's contracts with Gig and they are 1000% straight fool proof con game for the Greek. But Gig, if he had money, would probably give it to the Greek right now to back up his original sacred judgement. He is pitiful Mouse and there is nothing to be done for him because he is pathologically conceited and he does not tell the truth to himself nor to anyone else.

I am sorry about the Christmas presents. I got a very nice knife just as we were leaving France and it was my fault I did not write. Please thank Henny very much.

That was very funny about the double landlord slaying. Hope all teeth o.k. and that you have a fine time in Spain.

Feel bad to have written about Gig but thought you should have what straight gen I had. The Nairobi lawyers may have made a settlement with more teeth in it. Gregory's interests when he made the contract with the Greek were represented by the Greek's lawyer. So you can imagine what sort of instrument it was. I guess he was in such a hurry to get the millions he was afraid the Greek might escape or sell to someone else. That's why con men don't respect the people they con. The thing is that when I saw him in February he would do it again [WRITTEN: given money].

Don't you ever worry about people mixing you up with him. I have a brother too called the Baron and I hear, not from him, that he has just re married and that he and his wife are writing books together.

Tell Henny I met a very nice young doctor in the Army stationed in France who was from Baltimore and told me about what a wonderful guy Henny's bro. was and what a very fine man her father was. This boy had studied under Dr. Broyles.

So long Moose. Hope you have fine vacation.

[HANDWRITTEN]

Thanks always for the letters. I love to read about the hunting. Mary sends love. so does Rene and Bum. Look forward to hearing from you very lonesome for Africa.

HUNTING WITH OWLS

To EH, June 12, 1957
Arusha, Tanganyika

Dear Papa,

When Gig arrived here he told me how sick you have been and
so I doubly appreciate what you did. How are you now? Please
let me know whenever there is something I can do to help and I
will do my best to do it. Up to a point I have given up my old
"no responsibility" stand.

Henny and I only had two weeks together in Madrid when
her father got so sick that they thought she should come and see
him, so she went for a couple of weeks while I stayed in Madrid.
Liked Madrid very much although I think it must have changed
a great deal from before the war. Henny and I went one Sunday
to Aranjuez for lunch and then we walked through the park along
the river to the casa del principe. There were lots of pheasants,
all cocks I guess because the hens were nesting, making the
pheasants' version of a crow very raucous and feeding in the
nurseries where the soil was plowed and running across the paths
in the park. These, and the ones there used to be in the Casa del
Campo were about the only pheasants they have in Spain, too
easy to poach.

DEAR PAPA

Spring was no good for the usual hunting but I had lots of fun hunting alimanas.[8] Very much like Turgenieff. On weekends and public holidays I went with a man named Amadeo Marastani who had a live Great Horned Owl and two Ravens and we would go to various estates outside Madrid to shoot magpies, jays, hawks, and even eagles, though we never got an eagle, we did see one high up in the Montes de Toledo. None of the owners were ever there because it was the closed season, but Amadeo knew all the servants and keepers and we would go and stake out our owl and the ravens and either use one of the permanent estate blinds or we would build one ourselves. Amadeo was a real master at hunting with the Buho. He'd been taught by the Duke of Medinacelli and he took me to see his museum where we saw all the Spanish hawks and eagles beautifully mounted by Benedito. Benedito was certainly as good as Aikley if not better. We would call the magpies with a call made from a strip of cherry bark put between two brass strips. It makes the noise of the wounded rabbit and very effective. Equally good for rabbits, foxes, and lynxes. The best day I remember Was one Sunday up in the mountains south of Avila at a place named Campozalvaro. A granite country for grazing with sheep and dark cattle with black sharp horns with white tips. There was one good finca with quite a lot of wheat, but mostly wide open plains surrounded by granite hills. We started up on the hills with the buho and the cuervos using a small stone herders hut as a blind, but it clouded over and lots of hail, so we gave it up and drove down onto the plain to try and shoot a lesser bustard to show me. We could never get close enough and so we walked up some

---

8   Spanish for "vermin."

hares who were also down on the plains. A much finer animal than the jackrabbit, running like hell across the grey grass and then stopping and sitting up stretched full length to have a look around. We shouldn't have shot them out of season, but we only shot two, both well over two hundred yards with .222 Remington. Even so one was a female and when the keeper squeezed its nipples a little milk came out. In the afternoon we tried calling up a fox in the hills on the other side of the plains. Crouched behind a granite boulder squeeking for the fox there was a Wonderful view of the plains below where Avila was. It looked as big and unlimited as Africa. What it must be like in that high grazing country in winter! Like that mural of Goya's showing the farmers carrying in the pig in the snowstorm and the wonderful little dog. I think Carlos Tercero must have been something like Taylor Williams.

I saw the first three corridas of San Isidro, but they were not very good, cold, windy, and overcast.

I don't have a safari until first of July which is lucky. Have a really painful infection in the joint of my left shoulder, and it is taking a long time to clear up even with achromycin. Still it is getting better and should be ok by then.

Love to you both. I am writing Bum.

Much love,
Mouse

[HAND-DRAWN OWL] Henny sends much love Buho Kuss

A BAD LUCK YEAR

To PH, September 4, 1957
Finca Vigía, Cuba

Dear Mouse:

Thanks very much for the splendid, interesting letter you wrote from Spain. The Buho shooting must have been wonderful. All that is so much better value than the matan mas of the driven birds; although that is good to do sometimes for the practice in taking those partridges that pour over you flying contours down the draws and the fine high ones you get occasionally. Will send some pictures of some of that. I wish you could give me Amadeo's address so I could go out with him if you did not mind.

Gig turned up in pretty confused state at Key West. He wanted treatment and is getting it at Miami. I talked with his doctor again yesterday and he said he was coming along very well and had marked improvement after the first treatment. Am handling his hospital and Dr. bills and treatments etc.

This has been a bad luck year Mouse and please forgive me for not writing. I did not want to bother you with my bad lucks and figured you had more or less the gen on Gig. Probably much more than I had altho I wrote you what gen I thought you needed. Didn't hear so figured you preferred not to go into it which was fair enough. I kept out until someone had to step in.

Bum had bad virus flu and took no care of himself his wife having him go out to parties with a high fever when we begged them to have him stay in bed. Result very severe virus hepatitis and been laid up two months. Awful luck brought on by wicked management. Have been staking him too.

Mary is fine and well and send her love to you both.

Have practiced very severe discipline on diet exercise etc. Knocked the cholesterol down from 428 (very dangerous) to 206 (normal) Blood pressure from 200 over 105 to 138 over 68 (very good) weight down to permanently under 205 lbs. Today makes 6 months without a drink of hard liquor. All above very good for heart and all. You miss not drinking very much though and it is difficult on the nerves.

Denis is here for the worse fishing in 20 years. Wont describe it. Something has happened to marlin. He's caught one of 334 though so isn't skunked. He brought fine reports of you and Mary and I are both very proud.

Write when you have time. You can write or forward to Gig either through me, here, or Mr. Sully's address will reach him.

Enclosed the Warner's check too.

> Much love
> Papa

AND SOMETIMES LION

To EH, October 10, 1957
Arusha, Tanganyika

Dear Papa,

I've been out with a party since September 1st. A couple, Mr. and Mrs. Pierce from Wheaton, Illinois. He had lived for many years in Oak Park. A very difficult client, but a nice guy. He got all the big five, but had bad luck on his leopard. He made a good shot on him, but just a wee bit too far back and we couldn't get him before dark. In the morning, there was nothing left but the foot. The hyenas had eaten the rest.

Very glad to hear that you and Mr. Sully are looking after Gig. He was in very bad shape when he left here the last time. I don't know what the matter was and he wouldn't tell me, but he looked very worried and upset. About his financial set up, I don't know anything for sure, because he never told me anything and what little he did say did not fit together very well. I think that what the Greek didn't get, Jane did. I don't think he cared such, one way or the other, which is the attribute of a saint. I think perhaps that Gig is saint material. I can see it all in some future in altarpiece: 1) Gig, his wife, child, and nurse embarking for Africa, 2) Gig among bad companions, 3) Gig stripped by the Greek, 4) Gig bids farewell forever to his wife and child she is shown clutching two big bags of shilingi, 5) Gig among the elephants, 6) Gig going back: and forth from Africa to America like a soul flitting between the shores of the Styches, neither among the living nor the dead. I can't find any other pattern to his recent life but sainthood. I think Mr. Sully would agree with me.

Henny had quite a bad bout of the Asian flu, but she is well again now and enjoying her job teaching the third grade in the Aga Khan school here in Arusha. I am home now for a couple of months and we are very much looking forward to being together. We really haven't seen each other for three months.

Thank you very much for your check and news on the Key West place, Gig reducing the rent would make another good tableau for the altarpiece. Sorry to hear about Bum being sick. I know that party business is really deadly. I don't think I have ever caught any infection except when I was over tired. Yet a lot of that party business must be part of his job. I know it is of mine. The one thing I don't like about hunting is never being able to get away from the client from one end of the safari to the other.

You don't know how pleased I am to hear you have beaten the high blood pressure rap. I think Mary must have taken very good care of you and you of yourself, for that matter. I wish I could see you both.

I am a bit thoughtful these past few weeks as I am getting a bit fed up with Tanganyika Tours and Safaris ltd. They are a splendid outfit and Douglass a fine chap, but when you take out a safari in the field you are completely responsible for its success or failure, and the people pay three thousand bucks a month and you get six hundred. Would appreciate your advice on this matter. No man is an island etc, but isn't it better to be in business for yourself?

I bet Denis is having a good time! Does he speak Spanish yet? Tell him to be sure and not forget his old dolphin fishing companion. He must come and see us when he gets back.

The weather is lovely now, clear, dry, and cool and I have discovered a lovely little place in the mountains only thirty miles from Arush full of all sorts of game and there nobody hunts. I can drive out there in about an hour from the house and it is really something. The scrubforest is full of wild jasmine so that the air is really perfumed like in those Persian poems. It's on a ridge and you look down over the whole rift valley. Very much like Kitanga but has elephant, rhino, leopard, buffalo, kongoni, impalla, wilde beast, grant, tommy, zebra, and sometimes lion.

> Much love to you both and
> remember me to Denis,
> Mouse

I CAN BACK YOU

To PH, February 26, 1958
Finca Vigía, Cuba

Dear Moose:

My letter to you with the check and the gen on Gig crossed yours
with the new private bag address. Now when you get this you will
probably be out on safari.

Look Mouse when you have time would you write me what the
bust up with Douglass was about? The reason is that lots of people
ask about you, old friends, and prospective customers and for the
latter since you are setting up your own shauri would like to be
able to give them whatever you would want to give them. For the
customer would like to serve him something better than the only
gen I have "Douglass fired me in a fit of pique".

I know you hadn't been too happy about working for him and
were eventually going to set up your own outfit. But have sent a
few people to you and will send others. Any private gen you give
me will stay private. Anything you want me to give out will give
out. You are business now, not working for somebody, and good will
is one of your very greatest assets. It has a hell of a lot behind it;
all your knowledge, soundness, training and ability as well as your
skill with languages and your flair, but all these add up to good
will. So give me some gen I can back you with when people say
what was it happened.

DEAR PAPA

Seriously Moose that lion fight of Gordie's cotsie spooked me pal. Can you give it to me with a diagram that shows where the big gun was (the stopper)? Or just fill in the places you left out a little. Remember poor old Papa has heard the lion speak when he was not pleased and seen him run both ways. Don't make me have to wait to read it in TRUE. Never to belittle a customer or a client but did you ever see a follow man with a truly less inspiring face than Pete Barrett? He really had bad luck when they drew for faces. He seemed like a nice guy but all his stories end with the gun not going off or something mysterious having happened to the scope or something or something awful. Glad he has one that came out OK.

Let me hear from you Mouse.

Must get this off. Will write you a letter with all news next time.

> Much love
> Papa

FIRST SAFARI WITH PAYING CLIENTS

To EH, August 5, 1958
Arusha, Tanganyika

Dear Papa,

Thank you very much for the birthday check. Wish we could have been altogether for your birthday. Still, I know you had a fine time and work going good. All the best from us both.

Business good. I am off today to Nigoma on shake om trip with new boys. Have a core of very good ones, but any need polishing up for the first safari with paying clients which starts September 29th. From then on I am busy right through to March. Have been doing paper work, book keeping etc. until punchy, but has been worth it. Den was very helpful at Namanga, but there was so much blah blah main on, I never had real chance to tell to him about anything I wanted to. He seems happy. Everyone trying to marry him off to somebody or other, but he seems to be resisting manfully.

Henny has one month's vacation now from school and Elsie Blackburn is up visiting us from Dar. They are having a running cooking contest and I am reaping the benefit. Arusha has its drawbacks, but can get everything you need for good food.

Very grateful for Bum's help and yours. Jimmy gave me a very nice Write up in September Sports Afield. Will Write you how safaris go this year. Lots of western country closed for rinderpest, but they say will be open soon. Weather has been very overcast and cold, but last few days sunny and glad to see it.

> Much love to Mary and to you
> from us both

A TORMENT OF LONGING

To PH, September 20, 1958
Finca Vigía, Cuba

[MARY & ERNEST WRITE TOGETHER]
Saturday night, September 20th
Temp. in my room 82

Dearest Fellas

I've just finished reading Alan Moorehead's piece in the last New
Yorker (Sept. 6) about his and Lucy's journeys to the Karamoja
country and then up to Lake Rudolf and the Turkana and, quite
aside from the condition that Alan researches with a sharp,
sensitive and meticulous combination of eye, ear, smell, etc., and
that he writes with great apparent ease and grace (that's how it
comes out, I mean) the article has driven me into a torment of
longing that reaches out in all directions. Longing to drive a dusty
track among the thorn trees, to scramble if I still could over and
around lava rock with the tiny wildflowers growing beside it, to
look up and see an ear of Kilimanjaro floating free of cloud in the
early morning, to chat with Alan and Lucy who are almost my
oldest and most cherished English friends (we were all together,
comparative youngsters (26?) on the Daily Express before the war).
To chat, if I still could, with old companions such as Charo, and
NBebia and dear Mwindi, who must be almost finished now; but

MOST OF ALL to sit around and/or live around with you two. It is so, so long since anybody except Papa has chatted in the way that Mouse does, stretching my brain, cultivating it, and stimulating me to dig up odds and ends of knowledge long neglected.

And right now, before I forget, let me say, Mouse darling, that it is quite within my comprehension that childhood nicknames may not be suitable when one is a grown man, and that I use this only in private confidences, because it represents to me more affection, a closer tie, than a public name but in public I'll use the correct public name. (Puck named their dog, Bumby, and idiotically, it still hurts me. The dog is sweet and affectionate. They gave him to us, he being old and sometimes smelly now, and they not wanting him on their new move to San Francisco.)

And Henny, you dear rosebud I miss YOU. The way you flutter down your eyelids, and your sweet light voice, and your gaiety and your wit, and the rather awed feeling you give me that you are, somehow, an anachronism that your place in history is really beside the young Lady Diana Cooper, whose memoirs are now appearing in installments in the Ladies' Home Journal and into whose young woman life (about 1910) you would have fitted so beautifully, a world, as Diana remembers it, of flowers, bright birds, poetry a sort of diaphanous gaiety. The memoirs are much better than I would have anticipated Duff, writing from the "Western Front BEF" makes it all as clear as today, and despite her haphazard education, Lady Diana wrote her then letters and her now memories delightfully. (I keep trying to avoid the word "charm", it is so over worked, like some blasphemies in wartime; but it takes a bit of exercise.) I've got your color photograph on my billboard in my room, Henny, and I love it.

Bella Cuba has been an undisputed shit house, so we're going outwest (I think of it as one word) to walk in the mountains and maybe shoot a few birds and maybe even shoot a beast for eating. Papa bought me a darling little Mannlicher 6.5 in N.Y., and I want to break it in.

Pappy Arnold says the mountains haven't changed, and even if the town is overgrown, the air will be cool and dry. We've taken a house in the village (Ketchum) for three months, so will be there until just before Christmas unless it is too awful and Papa is overrun by autograph hunters. Just Ketchum, Idaho, should be enough address, and postcards, letters, will be most welcome. [EH INSERTION: (If Ketchum no good will pull out for Africa. Anyway will stay a month to walk and get in shape shooting so we can be in OK shape to come to Africa. Have had no exercise but swimming. But am down to 205.)]

Papa.

All through the heat and humidity Papa has been working like a trojan and keeping healthy weight down to 205 swimming to 3/4 mile a day in the pool. (me a full mile daily, until a Virus bug settled in and has proved about as easy to eject as that publicized air force rocket; but at one time I had 31 miles in 31 days good for the figger.) We are gradually closing in on the Virus (the same one, I suspect, that put me to bed for a month last fall) and I think that the general elation that will come with a spot of cool weather may boot him out for good.

[MARY HANDWRITTEN:] Best, best, best luck and a bushel basket of love - Mary [DRAWINGS OF BASKET OVERFLOWING WITH CIRCLES TITLED "LOVE BUSHEL BASKET"]

[EH HANDWRITTEN:] Best love to both, Papa

[MARY HANDWRITTEN ON MARGIN:] Gigi still seems to be taking courses at the U. of Miami. Mouse, have you got good clients, and how are the beasts, and how is the weather (upset, Alan wrote), and Henny, are you still school teaching, and what mischiefs have you been up to, and how ARE you? I'll be the cook and dish washer etc. in Ketchum, but I think of it as being a holiday with free time for letter writing. We have vague dreams of Spain next summer what vague or precise plots are you dreaming? Dear Children if I don't stop now, we'll all be asleep.

MY FIRST SAFARI WITH MY OWN OUTFIT

To EH, November 18, 1958
Arusha, Tanganyika

Dear Papa and Mary,

I'm sending this letter to Ketchum, and the name certainly brings back some memories. The Fall must be nice. Have you had your first snow yet?

Have just go back from my first safari with my own outfit. My clients were a Spanish party, two brothers named Simo Aynat from Onteniete, near Valencia, and I am now pretty well checked out on the Valencien dialect (a fer la man, chiquet!). We had a very tough hunt, twenty five days, but a nice butcher bill of two elephants, two buffalo, a rhino, a leopard, and a beautiful lion. Papa, I think you know how hard it is to do, not hunting in special area reserved for VIP's. I wish I could have had Pete Barrett along as leopard bait, the ignorant jerk. I wonder if would smell bad as quickly as a baboon or sort of sweet like a warthog.

Mary, I know how lovely Africa sounds, especially described by a good writer like Alan Moorehead, and it is lovely, but I think that there is only one Africa that is worth a damn and it's so hard to enjoy only that Africa and not get involved with the white people who live here. What a bunch they are. Only Simenon could do them justice, they are such masters of so little, like a milky film across the clear, cruel hawk's eye of what was once a really dangerous country. Mumo was telling me the other day what famine was like when he was a small boy in the Kamba country. His father was killed when he fell off a wild fig tree like the one you camped under while he was getting the figs for himself and family. Another food was the seeds from grass, which would still bear seed, even in a famine year. Mumo ran away from Kitni to the Tana River, quite a trip in such a country for a small boy. When he got to the Tana, there was no famine because the river tribe had plenty of fish and hippo meat.

Things are quite dull here at the moment. I don't have another trip until the 6th of January and Henny is busy giving her little Indians their exams before the end of the term. She says she is going to quit after December, unless they give her sixty pounds a month. Many negotiations over this. Think they will come across. The rains in Arusha are thinking about starting, each morning it more muggy and the clouds are very black by two o'clock, with some rain usually somewhere on the mountain, but we have not yet had much rain in town.

Please write me a short note with your address if you get this letter, so I will know where to write.

Much love,
Mouse

[PATRICK ENCLOSED "SAFARI PROFILE" IN *AFRICAN LIFE*, OCTOBER 1958, THE WRITEUP OF HIM AS A WHITE HUNTER]

A sample:

He started using a gun at the age of eight, and, once bitten by the bug, he just couldn't "let up." "Hunting is more than a sport," he says, "it's a disease you can't get it out of your system, at least not, maybe, until you're too old!"

CUBA IS REALLY BAD NOW

To PH, November 24, 1958
Ketchum, Idaho

KETCHUM Until JAN 15 1959
FINCA thereafter until End APRIL

Dear Mouse:

Your letter came today and was so happy to hear from you and
Henny.

It has been wonderful here since we drove out October 6.
Drove from K.W with Bruce like in the old days up to Perry, Florida
(now a big highway junction with fine motels) formerly the chain
gang capital of the resin country. Then by Mobile North through
Mississippi to some place in Tennessee and then up through Illinois
to Chicago. Picked up Mary there and drove through Northern
Illinois from Rockford to Galena really beautiful rolling and looking
like the Dordogne in France and sometimes like Bucks in England
across Mississippi to Dubuque Galena a wonderful beautiful town
you could see why Gen Grant was nobody there. Drove across Iowa
on N. 20 was a good road and then through Northern Nebraska very
fine sand hill prairie chicken country with the Sioux reservations
Rosebud etc. just north so town full of Indians at evening and good
steaks. Many cars with bucks on top shot opening of season in

Western Wyoming. Lots of flighting ducks and saw many pheasants.
Drove to North of Scott's Bluff and Torrington which are on US.
N. 30 and into Casper then north through Buffalo and Sheridan
and over the Big Horns to Cody. Next day through Park and down
new Super highway to Blackfoot and into Ketchum hitting Picabo
around 5 pm. We slept; out from Chicago at noon, one night in Iowa
in the Pfeiffer country (went through Parkersburg where Mother
was born) and Dyersville where my great grandfather Hancock
settled when he sold the Barque Elizabeth at Callas and brought
his children to US. walking across Isthmus of Panama to settle in
Iowa when still over run with Indians with the other Hancocks
had settled and one gone into Yellowstone country as mountain
man before Lewis and Clark. Was very interesting to see the small
English town and then the rich German Pfeiffer country towns.
I had driven Uncle Gus there once and we only went through
accidentally. What I wanted Mary to see was the beautiful part
of Northern Illinois which I hadnt seen since used to go prairie
chicken hunting with my father with a wagon and two pair of dogs.

Then we slept one night in Nebraska just south of the Rosebud
agency and the next in Cody. It was a lovely drive. Everybody in
Cody the same except, as always, many rummies passed away or
been called or summoned as Hailey Times puts it.

Here it was that wonderful fall things not much changed many
ducks (local) Northerns did not come down until the first snow that
was a blizzard ten days ago But main Northern flight still to come
Mary has been shooting very well on driven pheasant partridges
and ducks.

I have been shooting OK. Have weight at 204 to 206. Sprained
ankle day before yest which accounts for letter instead of valid
intention of writing letter.

Write 4 days a week hunt 3 and sometimes afternoons if go well.

Pappy and Tilly are fine and send their best. We are living in a cabin near the creek but have to shift to another Dec 20th.

Can shoot ducks till Jan 6th.

I want to finish book here go back to Finca, straighten up various things, situations and manuscripts there, do income tax and then go to Spain for San Isidro and stay there during the summer. Then would like to go out to Africa in the fall.

Cuba is really bad now Mouse. I am not a big fear danger pussy but living in a country where no one is right both sides atrocious knowing what sort of stuff and murder will go on when the new ones come in seeing the abuses of those in now I am fed on it. We are always treated OK as in all countries and have fine good friends But things arent good and the over head is murder. This is confidential completely. Might pull out of there. Future looks very bad and there has been no fishing in Gulf for 2 years and will be, eventually, no freedom coastwise and all the old places ruined.

Mr. Thompson is very anxious to hunt with you. He has the money to do it and wants to do it before he dies. Mrs. T. would be along as a non shooter. I talked with him about it and advised him to book far enough ahead and for a good time. Couldn't give him much gen as you had written me you were booked until next October. I did advise him not to book for rainy season as what they want more than trophies (those Kudu, buff, [EH INSERTION: Rhino] he has are hard to beat) is a fine hunt in Africa when it is good (where it is good) before he kicks off. Will you give you exact details on his condition and what he wants if you want them. Will see them when we go through on way to Cuba.

Mr. Sully is fine but lonely. If you could send him a card for Christmas he would like it.

We just had a letter from Denis. He is OK. but sort of gloomy. He really had a good time with us I think in spite of worthless fishing. Good eating and reading.

Thanks for sending the African Life piece. The guy meant well certainly. Pete Barrett is a true jerk. Old Jimmy Robinson is your pal. I might be able to work out a deal with Look that could do you some good but am always shy about burdening you with any tie up with me.

It could be a natural of a photo story But would respect your no or your yes.

Much love Mr. Moose. Mary will be writing Henny.

Papa. Weigh 205

See date on this for gen on addresses.

THEY ARE A HAPPY FAMILY

To EH, undated; postmarked May 12, 1959
Arusha, Tanganyika

Dear Papa,

The last ten days on the Coast I came down with the flu, thought at first it was the old malaria, but just bone acheing flu, but we still managed to have a very nice visit with Bum and Puck and the two little girls. The older one, Muffet, is already very pretty and much like her mother. Bum and Puck have a very attractive modern style house and I think they are much happier than they were in Cuba. I was very much impressed by Bum and how he has mastered still another career. Most people have only to be a success in one, and Bum has now two very much to his credit. They are a happy family.

Everything here now is politics and so complicated by the white, brown, and black business. All I know about is how it effects game. It won't be long now until the Minister of Natural Resources in Tanganyika will be an African. Whether that's good or bad I don't know enough about it to say, but it does mean change. The Game Department is moving this July away from Arusha down to Dar, for closer liaison with the Minister, heh, heh, heh.

How is Spain? I wish my season didn't start so early or we would both be there right now. If you have a chance, go and see the fantastic Giant Sable in the Natural History Museum in

Madrid, shot by Yebes, or have you already seen it? If it were only mounted in the same pose as the one in the Field Museum, it would break your heart. Papa, can't you wangle from the Portuguese Ambassador (the one I met was a great admirer of you) a collector's permit for two Giant Sable for a good museum? It's a trip I would love to do with you. I believe Angola is very interesting country, more so, now, than East Africa, the home of politics and the giant tourist seeing safari. The motto of B. E. A. is take all the tourist has and if possible give him nothing in return. The guided tour of the whore house. See how all the beautiful whores are dressed, see the interesting way in which they brush their teeth! There is such a thing as a "looker" in game too. East Africa is riddled with lookers. I have great respect for the good game biologist and nature photographer, but the mass looker is just vermin, like a herd of baboons, dropping their shit where ever they go. Actually, they are bored stiff by game after a few minutes, unless they can throw a stone at something. An African is fascinated looking at a lion, because he remembers how grandfather was eaten by one, and all they found was his head, with a peaceful expression. He is also impressed with the elephant because he can also remember himself as a little boy crouching in his hut by his mother's leg while his father went out and shot an arrow into the forehead of a giant beast that was eating his harvest of sorghum, which would mean starvation, big bellies, hard searching for bugs under the careful supervision of adults so they wouldn't eat them themselves for bugs, and death if the next rains failed. Much the same feeling you must have had seeing the Austrian in his native haunts. When he gets to know the elephant he likes him and understands him, not the bored, I've done it too of the "looker".

Thank you for talking about me to Marques del Merito. He
is your good friend and was very nice to me as your son when we
were in Madrid. I've just read beautifully illustrated book by Guy
Monfort (Sp) on Cota Donxana called "Portrait of a Wilderness".
What a place that must be. Spain is full of wonderful places.
Reading Yebes's book makes my mouth water. Even the little bit of
Vermin hunting with an owl (which is really a German sport) I did
with Amadeo Marastani showed me how good the Spanish hunter
is, even as an amateur. With the call made with the peel from
cherry bark he could call the fox right up to him. Has that disease
done away with all the Spanish rabbits or is it not so strong in the
milder Spanish climate?

[HANDWRITTEN] How is the Beria?

Must stop. Much love to you both. Love,

Mouse

POCKETS OF GOOD COUNTRY

To PH, August 5, 1959
Malaga, Spain

Dear Mouse,

Awfully sorry to be so late answering your fine letter but you know how Spain is and this has been a very rough temporada. First must tell you that we met the character you hunted with from Valencia who came up to Madrid with his wife. If half he says about how wonderful you are is true it will be quite something to meet you sometime. Another character named Andres B. Zala was even more violent in his praise but I couldn't decide whether he had really hunted with you or not. Hope he did. You have a very good cartel in Spain and I think it would be a good idea for us to be here together sometime. We'd have fun anyway. You could help me out signing copies of 'For Whom the Bell Tolls' in the callejon.

Antonio is wonderful, brave, consistent and unbelievable with both the cape and muleta. His killing is rapid but is still defectuous except recibiendo. But he does kill them decently and get them out of the way. I have learned more about bulls and the whole trade every day and it is wonderful to be back with it and have a chance to move around over Spain and make the same roads many times in the different seasons. This place where we stay is really lovely. Bill Davis is an old friend that you met at Sun Valley and we hunted jackrabbit together one time. Have been

to your place along the coast going back and forth to Antonio's
ranch which is north of Tarifa and this side of Cadiz within sight
of Chicana. That is a country that I never knew and you would
love it very much. We are buying some land at a place on the coast
in that area called Coinell. It is like everything was in the old
days before they spoiled everything. Wonderful beach, fine people,
real Arab town and good fishermen like Gojimar. Being around
Antonio is like being with you or with Bum except for having to
sweat him out all the time. He has had one bad one on May 30th.
and another that could have been bad but missed the femoral by
about a quarter of an inch deflected by the scar tissue of an old
cornada. He has thirteen cornadas altogether and not one of them
has spooked him. He is spooked sometimes in the night the way
we all are and prefers to sleep in the daytime which is smart but
he loves his work truly and he loves bulls too. We have a lot of fun
together, really fun and he trusts me very much and I hope that I
am good for him. There are a lot of worthless people around him
some very bad but we are sifting most of them out. We have run
into wonderful people on this trip and I have had the best time I
ever had and have excellent stuff for new appendix to Death in the
Afternoon which Schribners say will have the effect of a whole new
book. Enclose a few family pictures.

Also there are the usual problems of Rice and his stupidity.
If any bastard ever was shootable he is many times over but
I worked very hard for nearly two years without stopping or
interrupting and am in very good shape on stuff done or to do and
so can sort any losses he has caused by his negligence but I really
have to get rid of him after this year.

Hope you had a good safari and please let me know your
plans when you have a chance to write. Certainly there must be

a country where there are bad rhino that you can get permission to take out, when we think of the thousands that Jock Hunter destroyed for Richie it is pretty sad. Phillip wrote me that I would never want to come back the way things are now but I think there always must be pockets of good country that one can get into and hunt if we were not on the "big five" basis.

Love to you and to Henny. Will try to write more details about Spain another time. Never saw so many storks as this spring. Mille fois merde.

Papa.

GUIDING IS NOT PURE PLEASURE

To EH, August 17, 1959
Lake Eyasi, Tanganyika

Dear Papa,

I was very pleased to get your last letter and to hear about Spain
and all the people. Have you gone out on the sea around Malaga?
I only had a chance to do it once, but I remember how lovely it was.
Your place near Cadiz sounds wonderful, and you have the real
Atlantic. Do the swordfish run there?

Yes, the lion and rhino was a blow, especially as so many
clients want those animals, but you can still shoot three buff
and three elephant a year and there are a few places still open
with good lion, but the months for those places are June and late
January and February. I got two quite nice lions for my people in
June, one of whom was a Hungarian jew, but not nice like Kappa.
He had made his fortune in War Surplus. Never did a lion die in a
more ignoble cause.

I am now out with a party for sixty days (Jim Gay of Laramie,
Wyoming, and W. Wilhuf, from Miami, Oklahoma) and last week I
broke the half shaft on my Landrover and got your letter when it
went into Arusha for repairs. Yesterday we had a very good day,
getting two leopards just forty five minutes apart on separate
baits. Jim got his by himself and I sat with Wilbur. I'll be out until
the end of September, have a month's break in October, and start

the first of November with the Thompsons for forty five days. My last trip of the season is January February for forty five days with a Belgian couple.

Have some sort of infection inside my shoulder. It got so painful yesterday I gave my self a shot of penicillin last night and today it feels better, just stiff and sore instead of throbbing.

Henny went with me on the last trip and was very good and enjoyed herself a lot. She got to see us shoot the lion (on the 41st day!) and also one of the buffalo.

Glad you met Tony. He is a very pleasant boy and a marvelous shot, but as he says himself, he likes to do what is easy for him, and work, of course, is not always easy. It comes as a surprise to people, for some reason, that guiding is not pure pleasure.

Our next camp is way down south just east of the Katavi Reserve north of Lake Rukwa. We have booked a very good area and hope to get good sable. Mayito's sable country he shot with Roy Home is just about finished. Roy has aged a great deal but is still taking out parties. Safarilands has gone bankrupt. Perhaps Mr. Percival wrote you that.

It is time to go out now for afternoon hunt so will stop for now. Love to you and Mary.

Much love
Mouse

TO GO TO AFRICA AGAIN BEFORE THEY DIE

To PH, August 26, 1959
Malaga, Spain

[LETTER DICTATED BY EH, NOT WRITTEN IN HIS HAND]

Dearest Moose,

Thanks very much for writing so promptly when you are so busy.
Sorry to hear about the shoulder. What sort of infection is it & how
did you get it. If you can give me the gen on it I will write George
Saviers at Sun Valley to send you off some good new anti biotics.
He has turned into a really first class doctor & handled me on all
sorts of things as well as doctor Moritz. He was over with us this
summer at Pamplona and Valencia and doctored the whole outfit
including Antonio Ordonez who dedicated a bull to him in Valencia.
He would get the stuff out to you fast & will send with instructions
anything you need for your medical kit. Things have gone along so
fast in anti biotics that penicillin is as old fashioned & dangerous
to use, repeatedly, as something like calamine.

Tony seemed a good kid & is popular in his own town. There
is a big aficion here for hunting in Africa & I am sure you will get
plenty of safaris as it builds up.

Haven't had any time to get out on the ocean or the sea. This is
going to be a short letter so wont go into the many things I have to

tell you about things here nor about what I have found out about the shooting & fishing.

Would like to bring Pilar over next year & work out the coast & the currents around the concentration of the great swordfish & tuna runs through the straights. There is a chance we will have quite a good lot of money due to Hotch's merit work in T.V. & prospects of the theatre although the theatre is simply a gamble & there is never any real money left of anything after taxes. But once this years taxes are paid things look good if we have any luck. I am way ahead on manuscripts & the time I spent overlooking the last years is beginning to pay off in depth.

The bullfight season hasn't been as bad as 1944 with Buck but there have been constant losses among the characters who immediately reappear & get lost again. No matter what you read in the papers & news magazines Antonio is vastly superior to Luis Miguel & his sincerity, ability & lack of fear have almost destroyed him in the competition they have had. Basically it boils down to the fact that LM is spooked by bulls whose horns have not been shaved or cut down & Antonio can handle anything no matter how it is armed. He wants very much for us to hunt together with you, & for him & I & Denis to hunt together. So save a few beasts. He is coming out with us in Sun Valley after the season in Peru in October, any time he will have before he has to fight the Columbia season in December. Enclose a list of our fights coming up in September. Impossible to make them all but these are some good trips.

Please let me know about the shoulder Moose & take as good care of yourself as you can, I think you'll find that Mr. Thompson can't travel much & that Mrs. T. cant travel at all. So work it out on that basis. They will just be happy to be out there I know & you will get them some good stuff even with those limitations but dont drive them too hard or they will crack up. What they really want is to go to Africa again before they die & you know how to handle that.

Best love to you & to Henny.

[EH WRITES FOR REST OF LETTER]

Papa

What about that west Yellowstone Earthquake. Me cabra en Sos.

WILL WRITE FROM KETCHUM

To PH, November 10, 1959
Finca Vigía, Cuba

Dear Moose:

Send this off in haste. Will write from Ketchum. Hope everything
fine and good safari with Charles and Lorine. Give them our love
if they are still there.

Ein küss
Papa.

92 letters at the desk when got in 3 days ago

No secretary

I AM NOW WELL ESTABLISHED

To EH, April 11, 1960
London, England

[SAVOY HOTEL LONDON NOTE PAPER]

Dear Papa,

My season is over now until I go out again in June and then it is
right straight through until Christmas. This last season I worked
for 192 days in the field not counting all preparations before and
after and all correspondence and account which I did all by myself.
I take in about $15,000 but of course made only a small profit,
probably none at all counting what I lost last year getting started,
but I am now well established with lots of "good will". Africa is
going through a bad period but it looks as if Tanganyika may be
one of the few lucky places where it will not be so bad. It is not too
important anyway as I can pack up and leave whenever I wish.
No place is really fool proof anymore until we are all one color and
equally rich.

We now have our first real house in Arusha where everything
works, plumbing, hot water, electricity and have my pictures. There
are two nice Puis della Franca's down the road from here and all
the time Henny allows me away from shopping, eating, dancing
lessons and theatre, I spend at Kew, the National History Museum,

and the National Gallery. Most interesting time I've had was talking to the gardiner at the Australian hothouse at Kew. I am becoming a natural history bore but the beautiful patterns of cause and effect have men really spellbound.

I've just been reading "A Herd of Red Deer" by F. Fraser Darling. Very good. Ecology is a catchword these days, but the good ones are marvelous. What's fun too is to do a little of it yourself. What Henny likes though is Fortnum & Mason's, and I must say if you have a good appetite it is a good spot.

> Much love to you and Mary
> from us both
> Mouse

Back in Arusha 22nd

BIG NEWS FOR US

To EH, December 2, 1960
Arusha, Tanganyika

Dear Papa,

Business is very slack at the moment, and maybe over for good,
but I remember your good advice and I am not too involved. If you
have other worries, don't worry about us. Only thing that could
happen would be to be physically hurt in some sort of civil disorder,
and that is not likely right here, although Kenya is hot and will get
hotter until their general election after Christmas.

Big news for us, and I am ashamed you are hearing about it so
late from me, is our wonderful daughter who always smiles unless
she is too hungry, when she cries. I am inclosing some pictures of
her. Her name is Edwina, Tina for short.

Looking forward to reading the new book. International edition
of LIFE very slow in getting to East Africa, as it comes by sea from
England.

Just talked to Henny on the phone and she says Doctor thinks
she can go on living in Africa and go on safaris.

I am sending this to Ketchum, as Henny said over the phone
that Mary said in her last letter from New York that you would
both be there for Christmas.

Mouse

WE WILL BE AT KETCHUM FOR A WHILE

To PH, January 10, 1961
Mayo Clinic, Minnesota

St. Mary's Hospital
Rochester, Minnesota

Dear Mouse:

Thank you very much for your letter of early December. I am so sorry Henny has been having kidney trouble and the dropsy. It is tough for her to have that with the diabetes too and we send her our best love and sympathy. Mary and I stood by here for the call on December 30th and 31st but it didn't come through. Must have been caught up in the New Years telephone overcrowding.

The child you adopted looks marvelous in the pictures and you and Henny too. This is just a short note so you won't worry about me being up here. Had a 250/125 blood pressure which they have knocked down to as low as 126/84 and believe can be controlled by holding the weight at 175 pounds. Was 173 pounds this morning and figure we will be out of here about the end of the week. Will write another letter from Ketchum.

Cuba I imagine you follow in the papers but it is much more complicated than what you read.

I didn't think the Life pieces were very good but they were part of a long book which might be. Working on another book about early days in Paris which is very good I think or hope anyway, and want to get that finished now. [EH AUTOGRAPH INSERTION: Have plenty of other stuff ahead as you know.]

We will be at Ketchum for awhile. Plans uncertain after that. If it wasn't so close to the rainy season would love to get out to Africa. I thought of that last night and haven't had a chance to talk it over with Mary yet. Hard to find any place to work now where people don't bother you. [EH AUTOGRAPH INSERTION: and will let you work.]

I am enclosing the Trust Company check. Excuse this short letter. You write such good ones and I am ashamed to write a lousy one but I am hurrying so Mary and I can get off on a walk that is part of the weight reduction program. Address Ketchum and mark it hold and let me know anything we can do to help or anything you want to know about.

Best love. Mary sends best love to you both and to the new member of the family. Tina is a good name. [EH AUTOGRAPH INSERTION: Edwina too.]

> Love, [EH AUTOGRAPH
> INSERTION: to you both]
> Papa.

IF I EVER GET MORE SAFARIS

To EH, January 28, 1961
Arusha, Tanganyika

Dear Papa,

Very pleased to get your letter. Very impressed to hear about the weight. One hundred and seventy three is terrific, but I know it can't be much fun to have to watch it and keep it there. I don't know anything about medicine, so I can't help you that way, but if there is anything I can do to help to save you worry please write me about it.

We are having the drought to end droughts here in the northern province of Tanganyika. Business also is poor, so the weather fits the mood and the mood the weather. I have had to let all my help go, with the hope that I can get them back if I ever get any more safaris. At the moment I working for slightly built, elegant Hungarian with the making of Franz Joseph beard who has cornered the market in Germans, but luckily does not have a license, so I go along to guide on the "dangerous"(?) game. "Meester Hemingway, I have one fine gentleman next month, Graf Ripsnitz, very fine sportsman, you will like, he speak Englisch." Weidmann's heil! Weidmann's dank!

Have at last found the way to become rich without talent. Lend people money to pay their gambling debts at ten percent a month. You triple your money in a year, kill anyone who fails to pay. Do you remember explaining to me as a little boy in Key West about compound interest? I never really understood it then.

Henny is having a very good time with Tina. Yesterday she got her first tooth, and I'm calling her white fang. The only thing I don't like is that she wakes us up every morning at five thirty to be fed.

Papa, I don't know how much longer we will be staying in Africa. The trouble is I can't seem to make any sort of decision. What I know about is here. Bad luck, really, I should have picked someplace else to start with. Interesting to see how the elections go in Kenya. They are this month, and many people are very nervous about them, but my guess is that everything will go very well.

Write when you have the chance, and we will keep you up on our plans, which these days are always a little uncertain.

> Much love to you both,
> Mouse

THINGS NOT GOOD HERE

To PH, March 22, 1961
Ketchum, Idaho

Dearest Moose:

Hasten to send this. Have not heard from Bruce to write you
details [EH INSERTION: from K.W. nor anything new.] But saw
wonderful pictures of you and Henny and the baby that Bud Purdy
brought back. [EH INSERTION: Thanks for being so nice to them.]
N.Y. deal went through but had to deposit 70% against possible
taxes and may be worse but wanted to get this off to you. Trying
to finish book and things sound so lousy in Africa wanted to do
something immediate.

Things not good here nor about the Finca and am not feeling
good but working this may make feel better.

Papa

Everyone sends love.

A SPRIGHTLY LITTLE CRICKET OF A WOMAN

To EH, May 1, 1961
London, England

Dear Papa,

Thank you very much for the very generous check. Please don't worry about the Key West place. I am very grateful that you have been looking after it, and any time that you do want me to take responsibility about it, please just tell me what you want me to. I hope you get a smile out of this: how about making it a high class motel for negroes from New York? Our backgrounds are such that it might work and might be very profitable. It is already suitably zoned.

Henny has now been for three day here in the private wing of the University College hospital having her fact finding check up, and today we will probably know whether they will recommend any treatment here and now. So far they seem pleased with her and say that her kidneys have already made quite a come back since she has been on the pills and has kept her blood sugar down. The hospital people got us a good nurse for Tina, a sprightly little cricket of a woman, and we have two single rooms right together in this lovely hotel, the Cumberland, which smells strongly of cheap disinfectant and is full of dwarf young Irish maids who are commanded by ladies of a higher scale of diction dressed in black basic dress and also young. Tina is quite a hit with the young Irish girls since they all have young brothers and sisters that they left behind in Ireland.

I like London even more than the first time. I don't feel as sorry for W. H. Hudson as I used to. He had it pretty good.

Papa, if there is anything I can do for you, please just tell me what it is. I have such a good time in life that it makes me thoughtless and very selfish, but you have helped me so often and in so many ways that if there was something that you wanted me to do and I could do it, I would not feel very good about not doing it.

We will probably be here for another week and then back to Arusha, which is just an overnight flight by jet.

> Much love to you both,
> Mouse

ALL CLOUDS SCATTERED

To EH, May 13, 1961
London, England

Dear Papa,

We have had quite a long session here with the doctors, about a month when we take the plane back to Arusha Friday next week, but the results have been well worth it, for Henny in their opinion (Dr. Stookes and Prof. Hosenheim of the University College Hospital) has nothing to worry about her kidneys for a long time to come, and the very bad state she was in when Clara Spiegel was with us has shown a truly remarkable improvement since then, and she is able to stop most of the pills she had to take for the dropsy. She looks and feels the best I have seen her look in the eleven years we have been married, and it is, to coin a phrase, a triumph for medical science. Even my painter's eye can find very little to criticize in Tina's physical perfection, and we both hope that she will be smart too. We are a happy family, with all clouds scattered and blow before a fine West wind.

It has turned warm and sunny the last two days, and since the nurse has the day off to go to the Windsor horse show, we will spend this afternoon with Tina in her pram in Hyde Park and Kensington Gardens. This is nice if there is not too much wind. I never quite got used to the ducks not being shootable. Wonder if the flight would be so exciting if a person had never been a duck hunter. I love the blackbird (merle), and even the English sparrow is successful here, maybe because there is one just like him, much lighter in color on the Serengeti. The only one that leaves me cold is the pidgeon. That dreadful German "barbarian" they told me about in Venice who used to shoot the pidgeons in St. Mark's Square during the war, he must have been a naturalist. The only place for the pidgeon is Malad canion and the live pidgeon shoot. I am searching all antique shops for a "dog wheel", which they evidently don't use here anymore.

> Much love to you from us both
> and Tina,
> Mouse

Please write Arusha address as we are only in London next few days.

EPILOGUE

NOT VERY long after my father's death, all of the family was gathered in Ketchum. The primary problem at the time was putting together a funeral.

By the time we were all there together, it was well known that Papa had committed suicide. There had been some confusion at the very start about this, but by then the matter was pretty well settled.

George Brown, who had accompanied Mary and Papa on the drive back from the Mayo Clinic, was a staunch Catholic. And both Gregory and myself had been altar boys in Sun Valley.

The three of us went and consulted with the priest, the Reverend Robert J. Waldman, pastor of St. Charles Church in Hailey, Idaho, and of Our Lady of the Snows in Ketchum. We convinced him that Papa had committed suicide while of unsound mind. He accepted that idea. Mary, I think, was pushing her luck when she undertook to instruct Father Waldman as to what scripture he should quote during the mass. Father Waldman, however, did adhere to her request that he quote the scripture passage about *The Sun Also Rises* from Ecclesiastes: "The sun also rises, and the sun goes down, And hastens to the place where it arose."

EPILOGUE

And so, on the fifth of July 1961, Papa was put to rest with a Catholic funeral, conducted by Father Waldman. It was a closed-casket ceremony, which made up for the fact that no morticians could have dealt with the challenge of an open-casket funeral. What lay in the coffin could hardly be called the grace of a happy death.

Patrick Hemingway

ACKNOWLEDGMENTS

Patrick Hemingway would like to give a special thanks to his grandson, Stephen Arnold Adams, who was involved in this project from the first letter to the last, aiding in the transcriptions, discussions, and editing.

Brendan Hemingway: I wish to acknowledge my wife, Susan, for her patience and forbearance during this project. We went far, we went fast, and through it all she was always happy to lend an ear and opinion.

INDEX

EH = Ernest Hemingway
PH = Patrick Hemingway
Page numbers of photos appear in italics.

INDEX

INDEX

INDEX

INDEX